IMAGINE
· · ·

JOHN LENNON

Ima

ART DIRECTOR: NANCY BUTKUS
PHOTO EDITOR: ILENE CHERNA BELLOVIN

gine

JOHN LENNON

"Forward" by
YOKO ONO

• • •

Preface by
DAVID L. WOLPER

• • •

Written and Edited by
ANDREW SOLT AND SAM EGAN

SARAH LAZIN BOOKS

MACMILLAN PUBLISHING COMPANY   NEW YORK

Based on the Warner Bros. Motion Picture

Researchers: Laura Amelse-Luttrell and Frank Palmieri

Macmillan Publishing Company
866 Third Avenue, New York, N.Y. 10022
Collier Macmillan Canada, Inc.

Library of Congress Cataloging-in-Pubication Data

Solt, Andrew.
Imagine : John Lennon / written and edited by Andrew Solt & Sam
Egan : executive producer, David L. Wolper.
p. cm.
Bibliography: p.
ISBN 0-02-630910-6
1. Lennon, John, 1940–   —Pictorial works. 2. Rock musicians—
England—Biography—Pictorial works. I. Egan, Sam. II. Wolper, David L. III. Title.
ML420.L38S58 1988   784.5′4′00924—dc19 [B]   87-31761 CIP MN

Macmillan books are available at special discounts for bulk purchases
for sales promotions, premiums, fund-raising, or educational use.
For details, contact:

Special Sales Director
Macmillan Publishing Company
866 Third Avenue
New York, NY 10022

10 9 8 7 6 5 4 3 2

Printed in the United States of America

Acknowledgments

• • •

WE ARE DEEPLY GRATEFUL to all the talented photographers, interviewers, and collector/fans whose skill and dedication are reflected in these pages.

Thanks to all those who gave so much of their time and talent in helping us put together this photographic biography of John. I am particularly indebted to the following: Sarah Lazin, who, from day one, brought her strong creative and diplomatic skills to the project. She has been the driving force behind this book and it undoubtedly would not exist without her; Marianne Partridge for her diligence in helping us edit John's voluminous quotes; Laura Amelse-Luttrell and Frank Palmieri for devoting the better part of a year to culling John's spoken words and searching out rare photographs; Elisa Petrini and Barry Lippman at Macmillan Publishing for believing in the potential of this book; Nancy Butkus for applying her talent to the book's striking visual design; Ilene Cherna Bellovin for ferreting out so many rare or never-before-seen photos from around the globe.

I am very appreciative of the key roles played by the following: Yoko Ono for trusting us with the telling of John's story, for her openness and honesty, and for turning over so many previously unseen photographs of John; David Wolper for realizing the importance of this project, giving us his able guidance throughout, and for constantly demonstrating some of the best instincts in the business; Sam Egan, my dear friend and collaborator, whose insights and passion for the subject continually fueled our creative efforts; Elliot Mintz for his spark and intelligence from the very outset and for helping us to know John better thanks to their friendship; Sam Havadtoy for always putting things in perspective and helping us to find ways to make things work out; Neil Aspinall for his advice and assistance in our ongoing dealings with Apple Corps., Ltd.; Cynthia Lennon for her illuminating words, and for allowing us access to her valuable photos of her years with John; Julian Lennon and Sean Lennon for sharing with us their intimate memories of their father; George Harrison, Paul McCartney, and Ringo Starr for meeting with me during the final stages of the film and giving me their reactions; and Aunt Mimi for opening up and granting me an unforgettable interview about her beloved "almost son."

This book has also benefited from the energy and talents of the following dedicated individuals: Greg Vines, Julian Ludwig, Vikki Prudden, Kirsty MacCalman, Jerry Field, Ron Furmanek, Gerard Meola, George Speerin, and Vickie Hilty for their tireless efforts, and for always managing to surprise us with unusual photos or relevant quotations from John and other "voices" in the book; Rachelle Katz and Cheryl Wilkinson for keeping on top of the multitude of legal and business details that are part of this complex process; and Michael Ochs for not only opening his archives, but for introducing me to Sarah Lazin.

These acknowledgments wouldn't be complete without making mention of Bud Friedgen, the film's enormously talented supervising editor; Bert Lovitt, our very creative second editor; Kevin Miller, the picture's thoroughly capable and committed associate producer; David Gaines, the all-important overseer of the film's post-production; and Paul LaMori, whose knowledge and trusty computer helped us in our research for needed visuals and relevant quotations.

I am also deeply indebted to my brother, John Solt, whose face-to-face discussions with important sources in Japan gave us access to rarely, if ever, seen color shots of John, Yoko, and Sean taken during the late seventies.

I also wish to express my deep gratitude to my wife, Claudia, whose support and love sustained me throughout this project as we travel this and other long and winding roads together.

This book is dedicated to the millions of fans around the world who remain intrigued and influenced by John Lennon. Finally, I feel compelled to express my gratitude to John Lennon himself, who, having lived out his life as an artist, is an example to us all. John, thanks for the music, the message, and the memories.

ANDREW SOLT

"Forward"

. . .

John was a voice.
His voice went to many lands and affected them.
Sometimes like a storm, sometimes as a breeze.

His voice was loved because it was the voice of truth.
"You wanna save humanity but it's people that you just
can't stand." We laughed and felt good that he was saying what
we wanted to say but couldn't. It was fun to hear truth,
when you didn't have to pay its price yourself.

Then there was a time when the world thought his voice was silenced
by a gunshot. It wasn't. John is still singing. John is still talking.

His voice is a voice of love.
"I was visualizing all the people of my age group and singing
to them . . . people that grew up with me. I'm saying. Here I am now.
How are you, how's your relationship going?
Did you get through it all. Weren't the seventies a drag? Here we are,
well, let's try and make the eighties good. . . ."

Yes, John. The eighties was a real drag for a lot of us, though.
We did get through somehow. And we're all here, I guess. . . .
As I said a long time ago, "There is a wind that never dies."
I didn't know that that was you.

Yoko Ono Lennon
March 20   '88
NYC

Preface

· · ·

IT WAS A MONTH before the unveiling of the Statue of Liberty, but the fireworks had already started. As chairman of Liberty Weekend I was on the phone, trying to deal with a conflict between the secretary of the interior and Lee Iaccoca when my secretary brought me a note that Yoko Ono was on the line. My immediate thought was, What is her connection to Liberty Weekend?

Yoko assured me that the call was about something else entirely; she wanted to get together and talk. I told her that I'd be delighted to—right after the Statue's unveiling on the Fourth of July.

Arriving at the Dakota Apartments for our meeting, I paused for a moment in the entranceway, recalling that this was where John Lennon was senselessly murdered almost six years earlier.

I found Yoko to be articulate, charming, and full of purpose. She got right to the point. She felt it was time for a definitive

theatrical documentary on John's life, and she wanted me to do it. I wondered, Why me? Yoko's answer impressed me. "I want someone tough. Someone I can't push around." Her only admonition was that the movie had to be honest.

She went on to say that she had some two hundred hours of film and videotape—much of it unseen by the public—covering every aspect of John's life. There's little that excites a documentarian more than the thought of rare and unseen footage. She described film of John in the midst of creating his music, in verbal sparring matches with journalists, and in intimate moments with his family. We talked at length about what other elements might be involved; I thanked Yoko for her gracious offer and told her I wanted to think about it.

My trepidations about the project had nothing to do with the fact that I had only a passing familiarity with Lennon's music.

Having made over four hundred documentaries, I was convinced that beginning with an expertise on a subject was not the key to the making of a well-crafted film. In fact, I'd found that more often than not coming to a subject without preconceived notions was a benefit. Nor was I concerned that my own musical tastes ran more toward Frank Sinatra than rock and roll. I was a long way from being a die-hard Beatles fan. (At least that was so when I started the movie.)

My concern was simply that I wanted to be sure that we could assemble the material in such a way that we could reveal not just John Lennon's music, but John Lennon—the man behind the myth. When I began viewing the available footage, my fears were quickly put to rest.

Soon after my meeting with Yoko, I called a longtime friend and associate, producer/director Andrew Solt, to discuss the project. Andrew started his career with my company, and we had worked together on the movie *This Is Elvis.* I knew he had always wanted to do the screen biography of Lennon, and that no one would be more capable. Andrew's enthusiasm and that of my own children weighed into my decision. The more I read about John's life, the more I realized that his truly was a powerful story.

I took the project to Warner Bros., which agreed to finance and distribute the film. Over the next eighteen months, the production team pored over reel after reel of footage, from every conceivable source. It quickly became evident that the challenge would not be to find enough exciting material, but to confine ourselves to a two-hour movie.

I had tapes made of the Beatles' music and the music from John's solo career and I played them driving to and from the studio. Slowly, without my even being aware of it, I became a fan. My first comment on seeing the rough cut of *Imagine: John Lennon* surprised some of my younger colleagues. I told them that some places in the movie needed more music.

As I listened to the evolution of John's work, from early Beatles to the *Sgt. Pepper* era to his solo career, I was reminded of another visionary artist, my hero Pablo Picasso. Like Picasso, John was never content to rest on his laurels, or to limit himself to any one style. His music went through continuous changes. Like Picasso, he was a terrific innovator who always hungered for new ways of expressing himself. Boundaries were for destroying. Limits were for redefining.

One of the frustrations of making the film *Imagine* stemmed from the very wealth of source material available to us, from film, tape, photographs, and voice interviews. John Lennon's life is, arguably, the most documented life of the century. And few public figures have opened themselves up in front of the camera and tape recorder as did John. It was inevitable that not all of it would find its way into the final film. When it was suggested that we could take the best of the photographs and the best of the quotes and put together a book on Lennon, we realized it was a perfect way to expand and complement the material in the documentary.

In listening to John, or reading his transcribed quotations, it becomes obvious that he was more than just one of the most talented songwriters of our time. He was also a philosopher and a poet, and someone who cared very deeply about the important issues of our day.

I hope that through the film *Imagine: John Lennon* and through this book we have shown that John's legacy lives on through the music, through the words, and through the images that have been preserved for posterity.

DAVID L. WOLPER
Producer

Introduction

· · ·

I KNEW THIS PROJECT would be an extraordinary one from the moment I first met Yoko in her Dakota apartment. We were sitting on a comfortable white couch chatting, as puffy white clouds floated above us on a ceiling of pale blue sky. She wanted to show me something, she said, and popped a tape into the video player. Suddenly the screen went black and four piercing gun shots rang out—the beginning of her "No, No, No" video. The impact was chilling. An uneasy mix of agony and anger welled up inside me, and I was once again overwhelmed by the senselessness of it all.

John's forty years had been framed by intense drama and in the months after his death I began to think about his life, his gifts as an artist, and about making a film that would reflect the power of the man. The more I researched, the more it became clear that John had always tested the barriers, had always broken new ground, and had always reflected back to us his vision of the world. It became clear to me that what John was about was truth.

As a filmmaker and a Lennon fan, I felt his story deserved to be told in a way that did him justice. Along with millions of others, I had followed his life from the Beatle years through his maturing as an artist, his prolific solo career, his house-husband days, to his reemergence in the recording studio during the last months of his life. John—through his music, writing, and candid interviews—had always spoken directly to us. He talked intimately about what he was going through—what

new dreams, schemes, and attitudes he was embracing. Much of John's remarkable life was lived in the glare of the public eye, but it was only when Yoko sent two airline pods jampacked with films and tapes to our production offices in Los Angeles that we realized just how all-encompassing this project was to become. It wasn't until we began to sift through the material that we realized the extent to which John and Yoko had allowed cameras access to their private world.

Our task was to distill some 230 hours of film and tape into a dramatic storyline. Above all, it had to be true to John. So our approach was to let John tell his own story in his own words, though we have also included quotes from people who were important in John's life.

When David Wolper and I began to screen the first twenty or thirty hours of material, it was immediately evident that what revealed John best was the previously unseen material. John's work in the recording studio, in particular, sheds light on the evolution of his creative process and on his remarkable ability to transform personal experience into song. At the core of our film are the performances that go into the making of the *Imagine* album at John's mansion Tittenhurst in 1971, where John's compassion, imagination, and boundless talent become abundantly clear.

This book is intended as an extension of the motion picture, *Imagine: John Lennon*. We welcomed the opportunity to assemble a pictorial biography in which, once again, John's words would be the driving force.

In a way, it all began for me back in 1963—some twenty-five years ago—when I first heard that new sound from Liverpool. The Beatles' music was totally different from everything that I had heard before, from everything that had preceded it. A few years earlier Elvis Presley had opened the door, but now the Beatles had kicked it off its hinges. Ten weeks before their arrival in America, President Kennedy was assassinated in Dallas. As one era ended, another began.

On the night of December 8, 1980, another era passed. A peace-loving man who had given us so much, John Lennon's tragic murder marked a turning point for our generation. I am hopeful that this book and the film from which it sprang will strengthen our memories of John—a truly remarkable artist whose music and ideals will continue to enrich our lives for many years to come.

ANDREW SOLT
Producer/Director

WHEN ANDREW SOLT approached me to work on the film *Imagine: John Lennon,* I knew that it would be a labor of love. My only concern was that it would be hard to be cool and dispassionate on the subject. Andrew and I were both journalists by training, but objectivity, at least for me, I feared, might be hard to come by.

Call it cultural chauvinism, but I have always felt sorry for anyone who didn't grow up with the Beatles. So strong was the impression their music made on me that I often think of their albums as landmarks in my life. The memories and the songs are inseparable. When *Sgt. Pepper* was released, it was something akin to Moses bringing down the tablets from the mountain. A seminar on the economics of underdeveloped nations was scrapped as the professor opted to play the new album to a hushed class.

When the Beatles broke up, John and Paul were granted joint custody of my allegiance, but it was John's songs that held the most fascination for me. His *Imagine* album was as powerful, I thought, as anything the Beatles had done as a group, full of subtleties that only John Lennon could bring to rock and roll. I admired John's individualism. And I loved his music. When he died, so did a small part of me.

In the process of putting together both the film and the book, we immersed ourselves in hundreds of hours of source material, but it was John's spirit that guided us. Honesty was his credo, and it had to be ours as well. We weren't out to canonize a legend. Rather, we wanted to tell the story of a man.

John was an extraordinarily complex individual. In many ways, his life was like an enormous puzzle, the pieces of which were in front of us, but the solution of which was elusive. It was only when we began putting them together that a full portrait of John Lennon emerged.

Andrew and I agreed that, in a sense, we had to make our job as writers obsolete. That is, we hoped to avoid scripted narration. With dozens of hours of John's own observations to work with, we felt certain that we could weave together his words and those of the people he was closest to into a coherent and moving story.

While our primary focus was the making of the film, Andrew, David Wolper, and I all saw the potential of a powerful book on John that would enhance the appreciation of the movie. Images on film are fleeting; photographs in a book can be studied and savored. The same applies to John's narrative. The book gave us a chance to amplify story points in the film.

After being exposed to so much material on John, at times I got the eerie feeling that I knew the man personally. I had become so familiar with his wit, imagination, peeves, and passions that he began to feel like an old friend. Perhaps you'll feel similarly after experiencing *Imagine: John Lennon.*

SAM EGAN
Writer

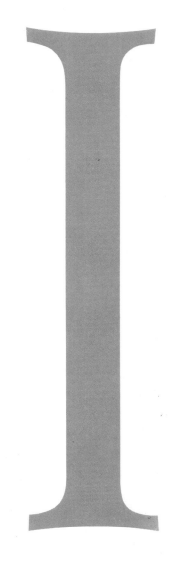

From Birth To Beatle

· · ·

Mama don't go,
Daddy come home.

MOTHER

PENNY LANE is not only a street, it's the district where until age five I lived with my mother and father. My mother just couldn't deal with life. She had a husband who ran away to sea, and the war was on. She couldn't cope with me, and I ended up living with her elder sister.

"My auntie lived in a semidetached place with a small garden and doctors and lawyers and that ilk living around—not the poor, slummy kind of image that was projected. I was a nice, clean-cut suburban boy, and in the class system I was about a half an inch in a higher class than Paul, George, and Ringo, who lived in subsidized government houses. We owned our own house, had our own garden. They didn't have anything like that. So, I was a bit of a fruit compared to them in a way."

—JOHN LENNON

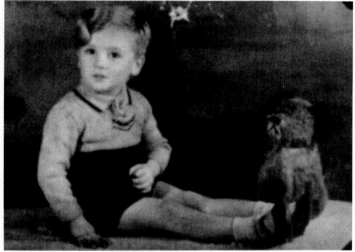

John Winston Lennon was born on October 9, 1940, during one of the worst bombing raids on the port city of Liverpool (*top*) during World War II. Throughout his childhood, John was shuttled back and forth between his mother Julia and her sister Mimi but eventually was moved to Mendips, the house at 251 Menlove Avenue (*left, as it appears today*), where he was raised by his Aunt Mimi and her husband George Smith. Nearby was an old estate belonging to the Salvation Army called Strawberry Field, where John would play as a child.

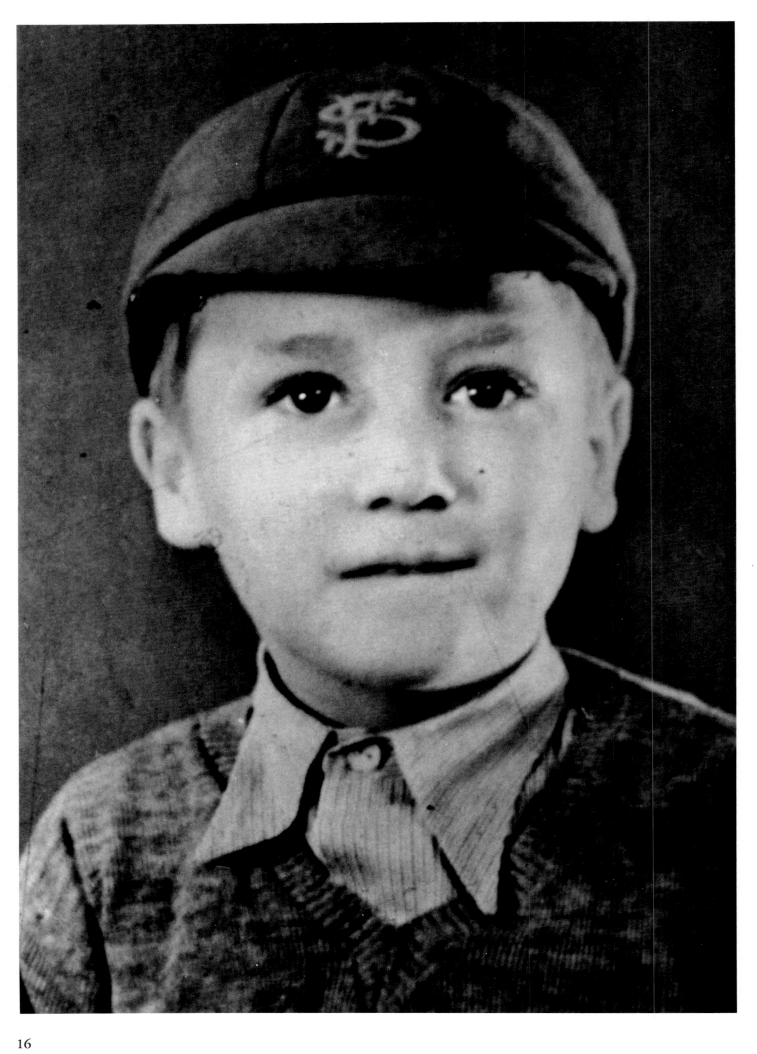

John's school photos at age six. He attended the Dovedale Primary School in nearby Allerton. Though he never did well academically, his Aunt Mimi said John was an inventive boy, making up songs from the nursery rhymes he had memorized. Later John would point to Lewis Carroll and in particular "Jabberwocky" as having a great influence on his work.

I USED TO SEND HIM off to bed, panda under one arm, teddy under the other. And he sang himself to sleep every night. We so enjoyed having him, they were the best years of my life bringing him up. I always look back on it like that.

"He was never rude, you know. He used to chat to everybody. On the bus going to town he wouldn't sit with me. He'd go sit at the top, and I'd sit at the door, in case he'd run out, you know. He'd be looking down at me and say, 'You haven't forgotten me, have you?' 'No, I haven't,' I'd say. He was lovely."

—MARY ELIZABETH STANLEY SMITH
John's Aunt Mimi

John with his mother Julia in July 1949 (*above*). When her estranged husband Alfred Lennon (*below*) showed up and took the five-year-old boy to Blackpool, she found them and returned John to Aunt Mimi (*right*). More a friend to John than a mother, Julia taught him to play the banjo, then the guitar, encouraging his musical exploits. He later recalled that the first time he heard "Rock Around the Clock" was during a visit to his mother's house. "She was dancing around the kitchen, saying, 'That's the kind of music I like.'" John was seventeen when, on July 15, 1958, a car driven by an off-duty policeman struck and killed Julia in front of Aunt Mimi's house. Julia was forty-four.

Alfred Lennon turned up again at the height of Beatlemania, publicly accusing his son of ignoring him. At the time John felt blackmailed into looking after a father "who never looked after me."

THERE WAS A KNOCK on the door, and it was Alfred Lennon. I looked at him and said, 'What is it?' He said, 'I want John.' Well, my knees went from under me—but he just collected John's clothes and walked out with him. So I was frantic. I found Julia, and said, 'Alfred Lennon has taken John away.' She says, 'I'll find him.' And she did. But fancy saying to a five-year-old, 'Who do you want to be with?' He didn't know. He hadn't seen his mother for a bit, you know, so of course he said, 'Daddy.' But then when he saw her get up to go, he said, 'No, no, Mummy.' And Julia brought him right back to me."

—AUNT MIMI

". . . I LOST MY MOTHER twice, once when I moved in with my auntie, and once again when I was re-establishing the relationship with her. That was really a hard time for me—very traumatic. And it just absolutely made me very, very bitter."

—JOHN

I HAD TO BE SOLID because I had a boy to bring up. It was my job to be there. He never came home to an empty house. . . .

"His mind was going the whole time, and it was either drawing, or writing poetry, or reading. He was a great reader. It was always books, books, books. . . .

"We were his world when he was growing up. . . . My husband died suddenly while John was in Scotland. And when he came back he said, 'Hello, Mimi, hello, hello.' We always got plenty of kisses. He had a present for me in one hand and a present for George. And he said, 'Where's Uncle George?' I just froze in the seat, and I said, 'John, Uncle George is dead.' He went deathly white, and went upstairs and said nothing. He never mentioned it again."

—AUNT MIMI

John, around age ten (*right*) and with his Uncle George (*above*), the closest to a real father he ever knew. George died of a hemorrhage in 1952, when John was visiting another aunt.

W HEN I USED TO get cross with him, I'd say, 'Now that's enough, John, pull yourself together.' And he'd stand by the door before he went to bed and say, 'One of these days I'm going to be famous and you'll be sorry.' Now, he was only about thirteen, and I'd say, 'Yes, well, until that day, pop off to bed.'"

—AUNT MIMI

"THERE'S SOMETHING WRONG with me, because I seem to see things other people don't see. It's the same problem I'd had when I was twelve, that I'd had when I was five. As a child, I would say, 'But this is what's going on,' and everybody'd look at me as if I'm crazy. So therefore, self-doubt was always there. Am I crazy or am I a genius? I don't think I'm either. . . .

"I always knew I was going to make it, but I wasn't sure in what manifestation. I used to read the reviews of books and art and music before I ever put anything out and I'd half expect to see my name in the review, even though I hadn't written a book or a song—I was expecting to see myself in news-papers, to be famous. I knew it was just a matter of time."

—JOHN

John (*left*), around the age of twelve, with Mimi and one of the boarders she took in to defray expenses. *Above:* John with friends Pete Shotton, Bill Turner, and Len Garry. John and Pete formed a skiffle group called the Blackjacks, later changed to the Quarrymen.

WELL, ABOUT THE TIME of rock and roll in Britain—I think I was about fifteen, so it'd be 1955—there was a big thing called skiffle. It's a kind of American folk music, only sort of jing-jinga-jing-jinga-jing-jiggy, with washboards. All the kids, you know, fifteen onwards, used to have these groups, and I formed one at school. Then I met Paul. . . .

"We met the first day I did 'Be-Bop-a-Lula' live on stage. After the show we talked, and I saw he had talent. He was playing the guitar backstage—doing 'Twenty Flight Rock' by Eddie Cochran. I turned round to him right then on first meeting and said, 'Do you want to join the group?' and I think he said yes the next day. George [Harrison] came through Paul, but the only person I actually picked as my partner was Paul. . . .

"I had no idea about doing music as a way of life until rock and roll hit me. That changed my life. . . ."

—JOHN

"HE SAID, 'YOU'RE GOING to the Woolton Fete, aren't you, Mimi?' I said, 'I go every year, John.' It was a gorgeous day, and my sisters were there, too. As we were going round, suddenly this sound struck—a thing never been heard near the church before. So everybody looked up. We were at the back of the crowd. And I said, 'It's John, it's John up there.' So my sister said, 'What's he doing up there?' I said, 'I don't know.' As I got a bit nearer, he spotted me. So he turned the words of the song into singing to me. And I looked at him and I said, 'You wait.'"

—AUNT MIMI

John performed with the Quarrymen, July 6, 1957, at the Woolton Parish Church Fete (*left*). In the audience was fifteen-year-old Paul McCartney, who soon became a member (*above*). The band's name came from John's school, Quarry Bank, and a nearby rock quarry where John and his friends used to meet.

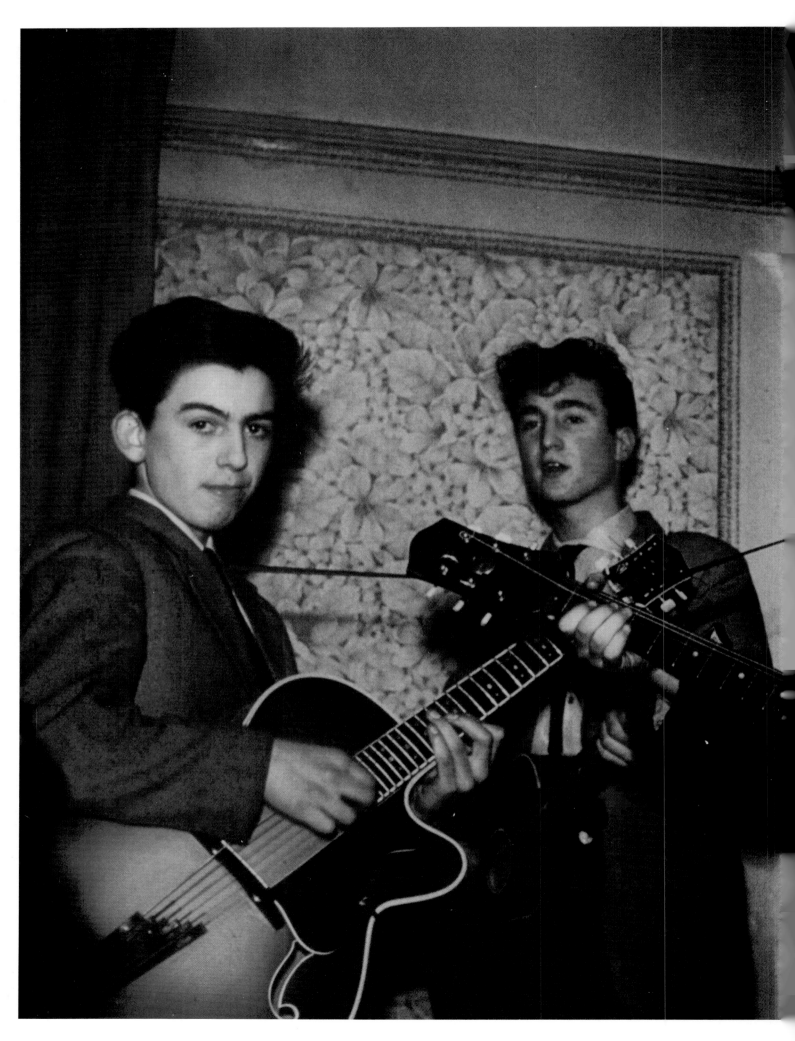

I ALWAYS HAD A GANG, I was always the leader, and the Beatles just became my new gang. I always had a group of three or four guys around with me who would play various roles in my life—supporting and subservient—with, in general, me being the bully boy. I was the one that all the other boys' parents, including Paul's father, would say, 'Keep away from him.' Because the parents instinctively recognized what I was—a troublemaker. . . .

"In junior school, in grammar school, I failed miserably. So the headmaster recommended me to go to art school. He said, 'If John doesn't go there, he may as well just pack up life.' So he arranged for me to go to art school, which I went to for five years and failed there, too. But I developed a great sense of humor, met some great people, and had a laugh."

—JOHN

The band changed names almost as often as drummers over the next few years, from the Quarrymen to Johnny and the Moondogs to the Silver Beetles and finally to the Beatles. The photograph at left was taken in 1958 by Paul's brother Michael just after George had joined the group. A year later John entered the Liverpool Institute of Art (*above*).

M Y IMPRESSION when I first met John—he was outrageous. At art school his work was innovative—totally different from everybody else's. I was an art student who followed the rules. But John wanted to break all the rules, and that's what made him such an individual and such a terror.

"With John there was an element of fear. He really quite frightened people, including me in the beginning, because of his attitude. He was rough-ready and not my type at all, to start off with. But this enigmatic character you couldn't resist.

"He walked around without his glasses, because you know there were lots of rough characters in Liverpool and, wearing glasses, he would be picked on. And because he couldn't see, he felt that he was being attacked, so he was always on the run.

"Even though he'd come from the middle class, his dress was very teddy boy, his hair slicked back with grease, no glasses, a guitar slung over his shoulder, and a look that said kill. . . .

"I think after losing his mum—which had only just been a year before I met him—his whole world had collapsed and this was his battle. He was a mixture of war and peace. There was a lot of battling, and the peace eventually came out."

—CYNTHIA LENNON

Cynthia Powell (*top left*), who married John in 1963, was a teenager when she met him in a lettering class at art school. *Below left:* Paul, John, and Cynthia with Ray McFall, owner of the Cavern, a jazz/beat cellar in the warehouse district of Liverpool, which became the main venue for the Beatles. *Above:* John, Paul, and George with newly recruited drummer Pete Best (*second from right*), whose mother Mona owned the Casbah, another popular Liverpool club where they played.

It was in the Reeperbahn, Hamburg's notorious nightclub district (*above*), that the group called themselves the Beatles. Paul, John, and George, in leather jackets and cowboy boots (*below*), Pete, and Stu Sutcliffe (*far left*) made up the group. Stu was John's roommate and close friend in art school. After Stu won an art competition, John convinced him to buy a bass guitar with his prize money. Paul thought Stu sounded so amateurish that he would unplug Stu's guitar during performances.

I was raised in
Liverpool, but I grew up
in Hamburg.

JOHN

The Beatles arrived in Hamburg on August 16, 1960. They opened in a cramped club called the Indra, and for the next four months worked to break into the city's music scene. That trip proved a disaster, in some ways—John returned home broke and depressed, George was deported for being under-age, and Paul and Pete Best were ordered to leave after alleg-

edly starting a blaze in their apartment. But they returned to Hamburg four more times over the next two years to ever-in-creasing popularity. These photos are among the memorable series taken in Hamburg by artist/photographer Astrid Kirchherr, Stu Sutcliffe's girlfriend. *Overleaf:* Pete, George, John, Paul, and Stu circa 1960.

HAMBURG, THAT CITY OF SIN! No, certainly not.' He said, 'Mimi, if you'll only let me go, we'll get one hundred pounds a week!' I said, 'All right, you can go, John, but I want you back in this house three full days before term starts.' And off he went.

"Well, a few months later, I woke up with stones thrown at the bedroom window, and when I looked out, it was him. 'Come on, Mimi, open the door, open the door.' And when I got down, he flashed past me like a streak of lightning, and he said, 'Just pay the taxi, Mimi.' . . . But I had caught sight of cowboy boots as he was going up the stairs. And beautiful cowboy boots they were. I said, 'Where's this hundred pounds a week?' And John said, 'I don't know, it's all gone.'"

—AUNT MIMI

"I REMEMBER THE TIME when one drunken kraut tried to get onstage, and John Lennon was eating onstage, and he threw his knife at him. And then, not deterring the fellow, John just promptly kicked him in the face to boot him off the stage. Stories like this were rife, because everywhere they played it would finish up in a fight. In one place they used to have to hide behind the piano because the pop-ular thing was to throw the chairs at the group. There were very, very wild times in Hamburg."

—ALLAN WILLIAMS
Beatles' booking agent

"IT WAS A VERY BEAUTIFUL friendship John had with Stu. John, even though he'd gone into the music end of the art world and left his art behind, he still desperately wanted to be a painter, and Stuart was a fantastic and dedicated artist. It was like John was yin and he was yang. Stuart had the discipline, the talent, he was a genius in his own right. John was the outrageous musician, whom Stuart was fascinated by, and Stuart taught John many things. They totally understood each other and gave to each other what they knew, what they had to offer. John helped Stuart to assert him-self, and Stuart helped John to come down a little bit, to be less abrasive, less harsh. That was the beauty of their friendship."

—CYNTHIA

I ALWAYS WAS A REBEL... but on the other hand, I wanted to be loved and accepted... and not just be a loudmouth, lunatic, poet, musician. But I cannot be what I am not....

"I'm not gonna change the way I look or the way I feel to conform to anything. I've always been a freak. So I've been a freak all my life and I have to live with that, you know. I'm one of those people."

—JOHN

"HE WAS A HARD KNOCK with a soft center, really. But most of the time he would portray his hardness, you see, because for one thing, it was fashionable to appear mean—the meanness that was coming across from rock and roll, which is part of the rock and roll image. And he certainly lived up to it. He commanded the stage ... the way he stared ... and stood. His legs would be wide apart, that was one of his trademarks. And of course it was regarded as being very sexual. The girls up front would be kind of looking up his legs, keeping a watch on the crotch, as it were. It was a very aggressive stance that he adopted. I can't think of any of the rock and rollers of the fifties who have that particular trademark. I always thought it was unique to Lennon."

—BOB WOOLER
Cavern Club MC, disc jockey

John on a Hamburg street. Fifteen years later, this photo by Jurgen Vollmer became the cover of John's *Rock 'n' Roll* album. *Overleaf:* To get the attention of club owners the Beatles had to *mach Schau,* or "make show," though sometimes John's insulting stage antics got the band sacked.

A RELATIVE OF MINE gave me a hundred pounds for my birthday. I'd never seen so much money in my life. Paul and I just canceled all the engagements and left for Paris, and George was furious 'cause he needed the work, the money. . . .

"I was always torn between looking arty and looking like a rocker. When we went to Paris and saw a different style of hair and dress, we picked up the so-called Beatle haircut. It was really trying to do a French haircut, where they don't have it parted at the side, but they have it parted high, a bit forward. Paul and I were there trying to cut each other's hair in that style.

"Also, the kids by the Moulin Rouge were wearing flared trousers in '61 and the round-neck jackets. So we went to a shop and bought one and thought, Oh, we'll make suits out of this. And they became Beatle suits.

"We just tried everything, and because we got famous, they said we were leading the fashion. But when we came back from Hamburg with the hair combed forward, the people in Liverpool were laughing at us. They said, 'You're queer, fags on stage!' And we had a hard time with the haircut. But we knew we liked it."

—JOHN

In October 1961 John and Paul went to Paris, where they celebrated John's twenty-first birthday. *Overleaf:* From left to right, Stu, John, an unidentified friend, George, Paul, and Pete in Hamburg. Though Stu left the group, choosing to stay in

Hamburg and study art, he and John remained good friends. In April 1962 Stu died suddenly of a brain tumor. Aunt Mimi later observed that Stu's death was "one of the greatest blows" of John's life."

The Beatles played the Cavern 292 times between March 21, 1961, and August 3, 1963, at lunchtime and in the evenings for around 25 shillings a session. Fans from all over Liverpool—tough rockers and secretaries with beehive hairdos—came to

hear the band. The club was a basement with three tunnels connected by archways. On the night the Beatles returned from Hamburg for the last time, almost a thousand fans crowded into a space designed to hold half that number.

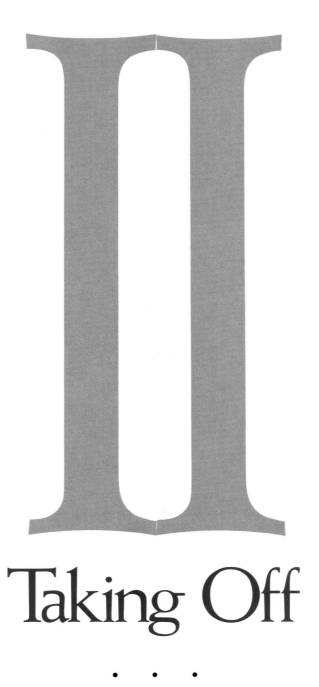

Taking Off

. . .

When I was younger, so much younger than today,
I never needed anybody's help in any way.
And now these days are gone, I'm not so self-assured,
Now I find I've changed my mind,
I've opened up the doors.

HELP!

D ON'T YOU THINK THE BEATLES gave every sodden thing they had to be the Beatles? That took a whole section of our youth—that period when everybody was just goofing off, we were working twenty-four hours a day. . . .

"First of all, it was making it big in Liverpool and then being the best group in the county, then being the best group in England. And then we got to Scotland and broke them in. Your goal was always just a few yards ahead rather than right up there. Our goal was to be as big as Elvis, but we didn't actually believe we were going to do it. . . .

"When the Beatles were depressed—thinking the group is going nowhere, and this is a shitty deal, and we're in a shitty dressing room—I'd say, 'Where are we going, fellas?' And they'd go, 'To the top, Johnny!' And I'd say, 'Where's that, fellas?' and they'd say, 'To the toppermost of the poppermost!' and I'd say, 'Right!' Then we'd all sort of cheer up."

—JOHN

The complete Beatles. This 1963 promotional photo shows John, Ringo, Paul, and George as the Moptopped-Fab-Four from Liverpool. Ringo Starr replaced Pete Best in August 1963 at the urging of record producer George Martin (*overleaf, right*). But the man most responsible for the Beatles' style was manager Brian Epstein (*overleaf, left*), who wanted them to project a cleaner image and tighten up their act. John was unsure at first if he should go along with these changes but gave in to Brian's sense of "super packaging."

Brian Epstein (*left*) ran the music counter of his parents' department store in Liverpool but had virtually no experience as a rock and roll manager when he took on the Beatles. He later said he had been struck by their music, their beat, their personal charm, and their sense of humor on stage.

George Martin (*above*), who had trained as a classical pianist, had produced every type of record—from orchestral to Peter Sellers comedy—except rock and roll when he agreed to produce the Beatles at EMI. At first he found them "a bit smart-alecky, like a fourth-rate Marx Brothers, but very endearing."

The Beatles and George Martin during an early recording session at EMI's Abbey Road Studios, where they cut their first LP, *Please Please Me*. It topped the *Melody Maker* charts in May 1963, and record sales soon passed two million.

B RIAN'S CONTRIBUTION was immense. I think that what he actually did at the early stages of the Beatles, nobody else could have done better. He really did organize that band. He was turned down time and time again. And when he came to me it really was the last throw, there was no doubt about it.

"His persistence got them into the big time. I think if he hadn't made it at this point, he might've lost them. They might have split up or tried to go their own ways. But he shaped them and gave them tremendous encouragement. He really believed in them. They were his babies."

—GEORGE MARTIN

"BRIAN EPSTEIN SAID, 'Look, if you really want to get in these bigger places, you're going to have to change—stop eating on stage, stop swearing, stop smoking.' It was a choice of making it, or still eating chicken on stage. . . ."

—JOHN

"JOHN WAS ALWAYS PUSHING me to push the barriers out a bit further, which was rather curious, because I was used to working with EMI, and I was the person who used to step over the boundaries, so when John came along, he was much more extreme than I was, and he urged me to do a bit more stepping over.

"We always think of Lennon and McCartney as a songwriting team like Rodgers and Hart, but they were each complete songwriters in their own right. Generally speaking, they tended to write their own stuff, but the influence they had on one another resulted in beautiful songs."

—GEORGE MARTIN

From the outset, John and Paul (*below*) agreed to share credit on songs either wrote; over three hundred Lennon/McCartney songs were eventually published. Though Brian (*above, center*) was closest to John, Paul helped him keep John in line.

When I was a Beatle I thought we were the best fucking group in the goddamn world, and believing that is what made us what we were.

JOHN

The Beatles at the Cavern. The night Ringo replaced Pete Best as drummer, a riot nearly broke out. Half the audience chanted, "Pete forever, Ringo never!" even though Ringo was a star in his own right, having played with the popular group Rory Storm and the Hurricanes. *Overleaf:* As Beatlemania took over, the Beatles stopped appearing at the Cavern. The band began touring the country, playing to larger, more fanatical crowds in established halls.

I WAS TOLD THAT he was playing his guitar in a place called the Cavern. I'd never heard of it. My sister Ann said, 'Let's go down and see if we can find it.' It was an old wine cellar that had been turned into a sort of lunch club for the office girls. When we got down there, it was packed. And there he was, singing away and playing—and the girls were shouting out, 'John! John! Paul! Paul!'"

—AUNT MIMI

"YOU CAN'T IMAGINE how big the Beatles were in Liverpool—not the world—but just in Liverpool. It was so big, I mean, you had such craziness going on over this band. It was like the queen had committed suicide, you know? You can imagine just how big that would be. Well, Liverpool was our world then. We never did get any bigger—all we did was get more countries. The *B* in big, as in big and famous, was in Liverpool."

—RINGO STARR

"THE FIRST ALBUM was recorded in one long twelve-hour session. We were in a recording studio for the first time in our lives, and it was done in twelve hours because they wouldn't spend any more money, y'know. The last song to be done was called 'Twist and Shout,' which nearly killed me. I was always bitterly ashamed of it, because I could sing it better than that. But now it doesn't bother me. You can hear that I'm just a frantic guy, doing his best.

"That record was the nearest thing that tried to capture us live, you know, and the nearest thing to what we might have sounded like to the audience in Hamburg and Liverpool. Still, you don't get that live atmosphere of the club, where they're stomping on the beat with you, but it's the nearest you can get to knowing what we sounded like before we became the clever Beatles."

—JOHN

P AUL AND I turned out a lot of songs in those days. It was easier because it was the beginning of our relationship and career. We had a little rehearsal in private, but mainly Paul and I developed our abilities in public. . . .

"But in the early period . . . practically every single was my voice."

—JOHN

"WHEN WE FIRST STARTED OFF writing, we used to sit down with two guitars and just strum at each other, and if an idea came out, just develop it up into a song. That was one way we used to do it, the 'joint compositions way.'

"And then with something like 'Yesterday,' I had the tune and the words. Or sometimes John would write them, like 'Help!' or 'A Hard Day's Night,' 'Strawberry Fields.' In other words, there wasn't any formula. We did them every which way, including loose."

—PAUL McCARTNEY

On their first album, John and Paul fought to record even one original song. By January 1964 the Beatles were a worldwide phenomenon. Working around the clock, record production plants rushed to meet the demand for 1.5 million copies of "I Want to Hold Your Hand."

It was like being in the eye of a hurricane. You'd wake up in a concert and think, Wow, how did I get here?

JOHN

By 1964 Beatle images were marketed on collector cards (*above*) and every imaginable form of merchandise. The group was mobbed everywhere they went. Once when John's chauffeur tried to stop fans from overwhelming the Rolls-Royce, John said, "Leave them. They bought it. They've got a right to smash it up."

WILL YOU SING something for us?"

"We need money first."

"Are you part of a social rebellion against the older people?"

"It's a dirty lie."

"Are you going to get a haircut while you're here?"

"I had one yesterday."

"What about the movement in Detroit to stamp out the Beatles?"

"We have a campaign to stamp out Detroit."

"Why do you think your music excites people so much?"

"If we knew, we'd form another group and be managers."

—BEATLES PRESS CONFERENCE

"WHEN THE BEATLES PLAYED in America for the first time, they played pure craftsmanship, meaning we were already old hands. We'd already done half the world, and by the time it got to America, the jissum had gone out of the performance. It didn't have the guts. Only the excitement of the American kids and the excitement of the American scene made it come alive. . . ."

—JOHN

"THE NOISE AT THE AIRPORT—we all thought the screaming was the screaming of the jet engines, but in fact it was the screaming of the fans. I had to keep a low profile, because it wouldn't do for the frenzied fans to know that John had a wife and a baby at home."

—CYNTHIA

Five thousand fans greeted the Beatles when they landed in New York, February 7, 1964, to appear on "The Ed Sullivan Show." The first night they performed (*above*), before a record-setting television audience of 70 million Americans, the national crime rate dropped dramatically for a few hours.

In New York the line of fans waiting to see the Beatles stretched three blocks from their hotel (*left*). Cassius Clay invited them to watch a future champ train (*above*). Even a stroll along a beach in Miami turned into a media event (*below*). John (*overleaf*) had a few quiet moments on the train trip to Washington, D.C., the site of their first American concert.

I WAS GOING HOME in the car from a day's work with Dick Lester and he said, 'We're gonna use the title 'A Hard Day's Night,' which was something Ringo had said—just an off-the-cuff remark. And the next morning, I brought in the song. . . .

"*A Hard Day's Night* was a comic-strip version of what actually was going on. It wasn't that care-free ever. The pressure was far heavier than that. It was written after the author spent three days with us when we played in London and Dublin. He wrote the whole film based on our characters. You know, clodhopping Ringo, sharp John, whimsical Paul, and stern George. And all the Beatle character myths were formed from three days of watching us, which was a lot of junk, really."

—JOHN

The Beatles' first film, *A Hard Day's Night,* premiered the summer of 1964 in London's Piccadilly Circus (*above*). A black and white fictionalized documentary, the film (*right*) was based, according to director Richard Lester, on the private and public constraints of the Beatles' celebrity.

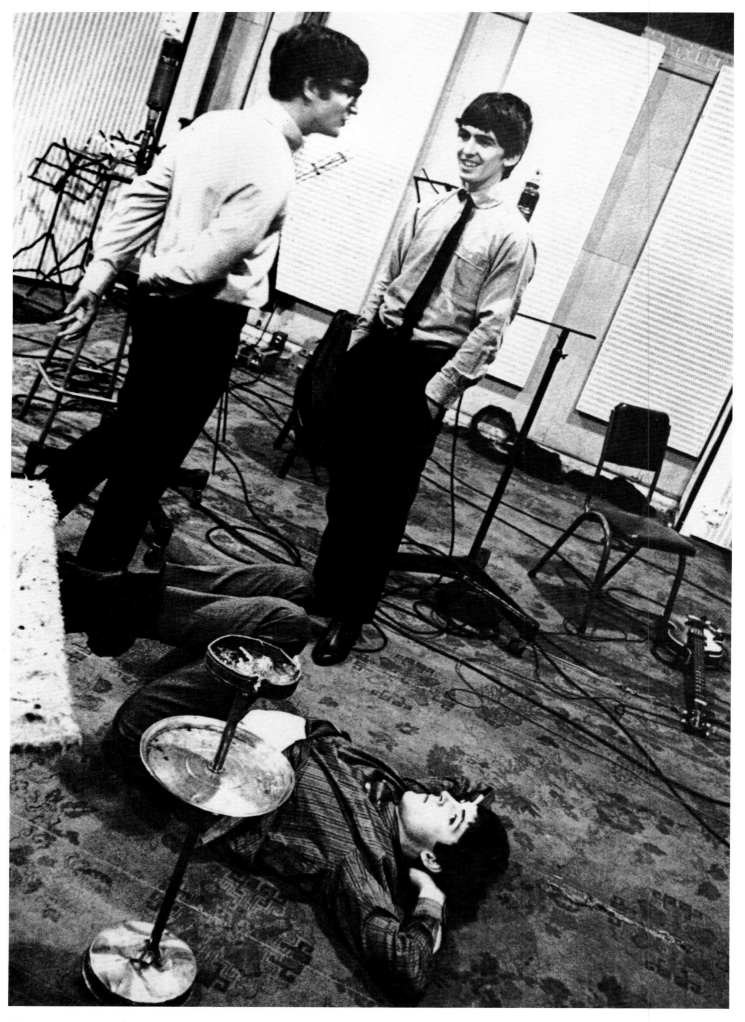

A Hard Day's Night was a box-office success, as fans thronged to see it dozens of times. Meanwhile, the Beatles began a prolific period of writing and recording. From 1964 through 1966, they released twelve albums in America and five in Great Britain, including *Help!, Rubber Soul,* and *Revolver,* which featured all original Beatles compositions.

John became known as the "intelligent" Beatle when he published his first book in England in March 1964. This series of photos was taken for the cover of *In His Own Write,* a collection of poems and drawings. Not only was it a popular success, selling over 100,000 copies, but it was critically acclaimed as well. John was toasted by the literary establishment at a well-attended luncheon at the Dorchester Hotel. A second volume, *A Spaniard in the Works,* appeared a year later.

EVERYBODY AT THE SAME TIME was finding out . . . that the values didn't mean a thing, you know, and you could make it without college and education and all those things. It's nice to be able to read and write but, apart from that, I never learned anything worth a damn . . . in school.

"When it started with me, George, Paul, and Ringo, we said, 'Listen, man,' you know, 'here's a field of professionalism that doesn't need any qualifications except you gotta get down to it, you know, and wanna do it. You can make it in the terms of the world. You can make it without that pressure.'"

—JOHN

INTERVIEWER: "Living in the butterfly world of pop as a Beatle, do you find that this undermines people's serious acceptance of you as a writer?"

John: "Ah, it does, but I didn't really expect them to take me seriously. They do take it more seriously than I thought, so that's good enough for me. In the old days I used to think songwriting is this: I love you and you love me. And my writing was something else, even if I didn't think of it quite like that. Now, I've just realized through Dylan and other people—Bob Dylan, not Thomas—it is the same thing."

Interviewer: "Have you been writing lately?"

John: "Well, I write—I think all the time, so I mean, it's the same. I actually don't put it on paper so much these days, but it goes into songs—a lot of the same energy that went into those poems. The thoughts come out either on film or on paper, or on tape. I've just got lots of tape, which if I put onto paper it would be a book. I mean, it's just a matter of do I want to make those tapes into paper or make the tapes into records."

—FROM A BBC INTERVIEW

Work is life, you know, and without it, there's nothing but fear and insecurity.

JOHN

T HE IDEA OF BEING a rock and roll musician sort of suited my talents and mentality. The freedom was great, but then I found out I wasn't free. I'd got boxed in. . . . The whole Beatle thing was just beyond comprehension. And I was eating and drinking like a pig, and I was fat as a pig, dissatisfied with myself, and subconsciously was crying for help."

—JOHN

The Beatles on location in the Bahamas for *Help!* (right), their second movie. Director Richard Lester decided to change the name of the film from *Eight Arms to Hold You* when John showed him the lyrics to a song he had just written, titled "Help!" John, who was beginning to chafe under the rigors of Beatlemania, later referred to this time as his "fat Elvis" period. This premiere program (*above*) was signed by the four Beatles for one of the film's co-stars, Victor Spinetti.

BRIAN WANTED DESPERATELY to make good for [the Beatles]. His wonderful flair made it possible for all of them to actually become superstars. He had the dream that they had, but he knew how to put it into action. Musicians are notoriously hopeless at business and money and handling things. He wanted to clean them up for his promotion, which at first John balked against—you know, the Beatles suits and the haircuts and everything—but their relationship was very good. It was a lovely relationship."

—CYNTHIA

"I WAS ON HOLIDAY with Brian Epstein in Spain, where the rumors went round that he and I were having a love affair. Well, it was almost a love affair but not quite. It was never consummated but it was a pretty intense relationship. It was my first experience spending time with a homosexual. We left Cyn with the baby, and I went to Spain and we had lots of funny stories, you know. We used to sit in the cafés, looking at all the boys. And I'd say, 'Do you like that one? Do you like this one?' I was sort of enjoying the experience, all the time thinking like a writer."

—JOHN

The Beatles' fame even won the attention of the royal family. In 1964 they were greeted by Princess Margaret (*above, right*) and a year later (*left*, with Brian Epstein) were awarded the M.B.E. (Member of the Most Excellent Order of the British Empire), one of the nation's most coveted civilian honors. In 1969 John returned the decoration, protesting the British government's policies in Biafra and its support of U.S. involvement in Vietnam.

Cynthia (*left*), in perfect Carnaby Street gear, followed the rules for being the model rock and roll wife—as she put it: "Steer clear of the press, keep out of the way, and 'I love you regard-less.'" *Above:* Cynthia and John in Florida after the first U.S. tour; (*below, left*) with their son Julian, born April 8, 1963, and (*right*) on holiday with Ringo and his wife Maureen.

J
OHN AS A FATHER was forced, I'm afraid, to be a part-time dad. For the first few years when we saw him it was between tours and recording albums. He would sleep until late and be up until late, so when he saw Julian he was lovely. Bemused, I think, because he didn't quite understand that this little boy was his. As Julian got older, John became more emotional about being a father. There was a period, '64, '65, when he wrote to me saying, 'I'm so sad and I'm so sorry that I've missed the fact that Julian has been growing up, that he is now a little man and I miss him dreadfully and I've been a right bastard because I've taken no notice of him or I've read the papers and pushed him out of the room because he's been making noise.' It hit John on this particular tour. I think he took a very strong look inside himself and saw what he'd been missing."

—CYNTHIA

In July 1964 John and Cynthia moved into Weybridge (*top*), an elegant house in Kenwood's "stockbroker belt" near London. John converted a top-floor room into a painting studio (*above*). *Right:* John poses behind a suit of armor in the entrance hall.

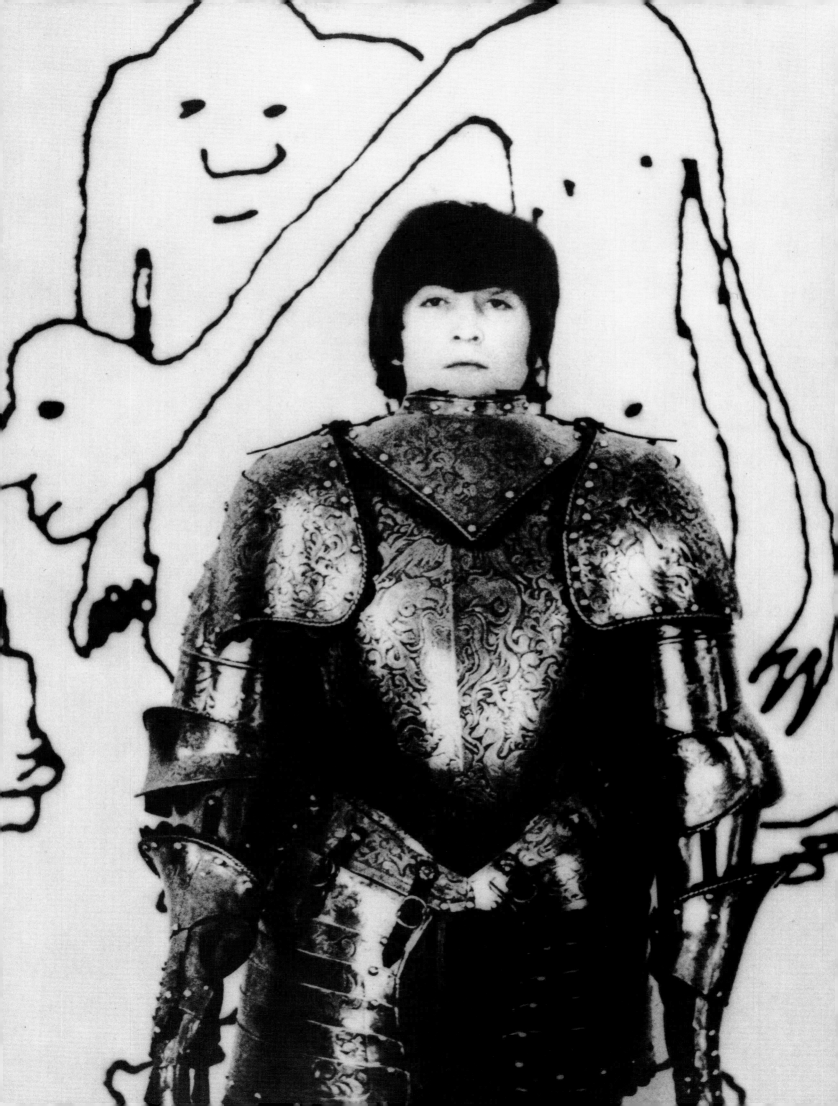

Between world tours John, Cynthia, and Julian had very little time for family life despite these whimsical portraits taken in the summer of 1965. The pressure of Beatlemania became almost unbearable to John, and though Weybridge was a haven, he also described it as "like a bus stop, you wait until something comes along."

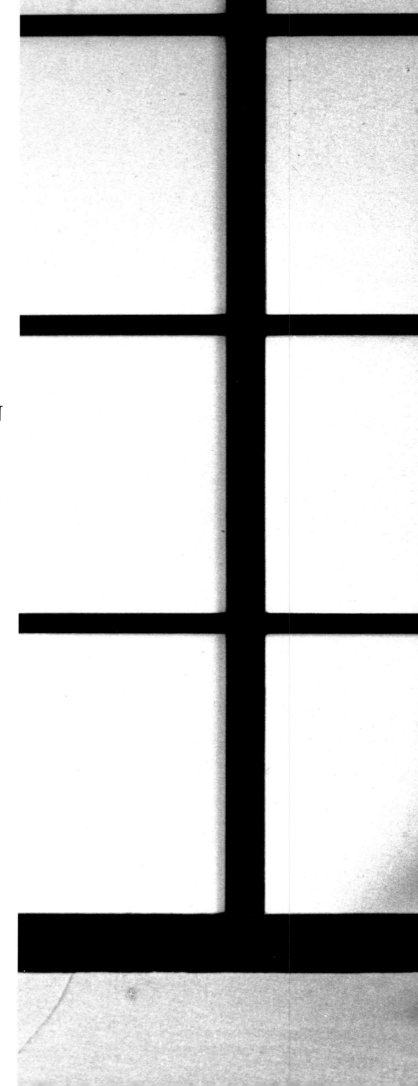

My defenses were so great. The cocky rock and roll hero who knows all the answers was actually a terrified guy who didn't know how to cry. Simple.

JOHN

Trouble At The Top

· · ·

I read the news today, oh boy,
About a lucky man who made the grade.
And though the news was rather sad,
Well, I just had to laugh.

A DAY IN THE LIFE

CHRISTIANITY WILL GO. It will vanish and shrink. I needn't argue with that; I'm right and I will be proved right. We're more popular than Jesus now; I don't know which will go first—rock and roll or Christianity. Jesus was all right, but his disciples were thick and ordinary. It's them twisting it that ruins it for me."

—JOHN

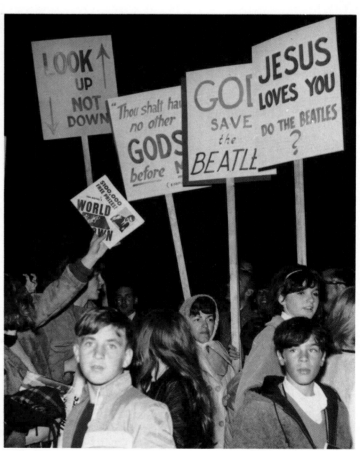

In February 1966 reporter Maureen Cleave, a friend of John's, published a candid interview with him. Included was John's view of the current state of religion: "Christianity will go. . . . We're more popular than Jesus now. . . ." Reactions in the United States ranged from banning the group's music to Ku Klux Klan marches and public bonfires burning Beatle records (*previous page*). Brian immediately arranged a press conference (*left*), though John had to be cajoled into apologizing. Tommy Charles (*above*), an Alabama disc jockey, led southern Bible Belt protests.

T HE STATEMENT about the Beatles being more popular than Jesus caused John tremendous pain. In many ways, I don't think John as a Beatle ever recovered from the impact. It represented to some degree the end of the love relationship between the Beatles and the press. After that year the press pounced on them, and it was never the same."

—ELLIOT MINTZ
Media consultant and John's friend

"I'M NOT SAYING that we're better or greater, or comparing us with Jesus Christ as a person, or God as a thing, or whatever it is. I just said what I said, and it was wrong, or it was taken wrong. And now it's all this."

—JOHN

Even after numerous explanations and apologies by John (*above*), opinion on Lennon's Christ comment was still divided. At concerts a strong show of Beatle support countered the backlash. *Left:* Fans at San Francisco's Candlestick Park rallied to Lennon's defense.

THE 1966 TOUR was a watershed for John and the rest of the group. He went through a terrible period of aggravation and hate. He wondered, Why do people take me so seriously because of one statement that was taken out of context? So, I think at that point he decided it was time to step back and let Paul take over more."
—CYNTHIA

"IT GOT A LITTLE BORING. I mean, it was great when it first happened, but then it just became like lip-synching, miming. Sometimes things would break down and nobody would know. And it wasn't doing the music any good. . . . The music wasn't being heard. It was just a sort of a freak show. The Beatles were the show, and the music had nothing to do with it. Since we were musicians, we felt there was no enjoyment in it. The only reason to be Beatles is to make music, and not just be in a circus."

—JOHN

In the summer of 1966 the Beatles began a problem-plagued world tour. In addition to the difficulties caused by the Christ comment, there were riots in the Philippines when the Beatles allegedly snubbed President Ferdinand Marcos's wife Imelda by not attending a party. The performance at Candlestick Park, San Francisco, on August 29 (*left and above*) turned out to be their last concert appearance.

After three years of almost constant touring, the Beatles turned to individual projects. John worked with Richard Lester in *How I Won the War (left)*, an antiwar film. On location in Spain, John wrote "Strawberry Fields Forever." John, as Private Gripweed *(below)*, was on the first cover of *Rolling Stone* magazine, wearing the glasses that were to become his trademark.

AFTER THE BEATLES' LAST TOUR I was dead nervous, so I said yes to Dick Lester because I didn't know what to do. What do you do when you don't tour, there's no life. So . . . I did the movie, but I was thinking, Well, this is the end, really, you know. There's going to be a blank space in the future. That's when I really started considering life without the Beatles—when I started thinking about it. But I could not think what it would be, or how I could do it. I didn't consider forming my own group or anything, because it didn't even enter my mind. Just, What would I do when it stopped?"

—JOHN

NOVEMBER 9, 1967
VOL. I, NO. 1

OUR PRICE:
TWENTY-FIVE CENTS

MFP

IN THIS ISSUE:

Tom Rounds Quits KFRC

Tom Rounds, KFRC Program Director, has resigned. No immediate date has been set for his departure from the station. Rounds quit to assume the direction of Charlatan Productions, an L.A. based film company experimenting in the contemporary pop film.

Rounds spent seven years as Program Director of KPOI in Hawaii before coming to San Francisco in 1966. He successfully effected the tight format which made KFRC the number one station in San Francisco.

Les Turpin, former program director of KGB in San Diego will replace Tom Rounds at KFRC. Turpin has spent the last year as a consultant in the Drake-Chenault programming service.

The new appointment could mean a tightening up of programming policies. Rounds liberalization of KFRC's play-list may well become more restricted.

Recognize Private Gripweed? He's actually John Lennon in Richard Lester's new film, How I Won the War. An illustrated special preview of the movie begins on page 16.

THE HIGH COST OF MUSIC AND LOVE: WHERE'S THE MONEY FROM MONTEREY?

BY MICHAEL LYDON

A weekend of "music, love, and flowers" can be done for a song (plus cost) or can be done at a cost (plus songs). The Monterey International Pop Festival, a non-profit, charity event, was, despite its own protestations, of the second sort: a damn extravagant three days.

The Festival's net profit at the end of August, the last date of accounting, was $211,451. The costs of the weekend were $290,233. Had it not been for the profit from the sale of television rights to ABC-TV of $288,843, the whole operation would have ended up a neat $77,392 in the red.

The Festival planned to have all the artists, while in Monterey, submit ideas for use of the proceeds.

In the confusion the plan miscarried and the decision on where the profits should go has still not been finally made.

So far only $50,000 has definitely been been allocated to

anyone: to a unit of the New York City Youth Board which will set up classes for many ghetto children to learn music on guitars donated by Fender. Paul Simon, a Festival governor, will personally over see the program.

Plans to give more money to the Negro College Fund for college scholarships is now being discussed; another idea is a sum between ten and twenty thousand for the Monterey Symphony.

However worthy these plans, they are considerably less daring and innovative than the projects mentioned in the spring: the Diggers, pop conferences, and any project which would "tend to further national interest in and knowledge and enjoyment of popular music." The present plans suggest that the Board of Governors, unable or unwilling to make their grandiose schemes reality, fell back on traditional charity.

The Board of Governors did decide that the money would be given out in a small number of

large sums. This has meant, for instance, that the John Edwards Memorial Foundation, a folk music archive at the University of California at Los Angeles, had its small request overlooked.

In ironic fact, what happened at the Festival and its financial affairs looks in many ways like the traditional Charity Ball in hippie drag.

The overhead was high and the net was low. "For every dollar spent, there was a reason," says Derek Taylor, the Festival's PR man and one of its original officers.

Yet many of the Festival's expenses, however reasonable to Taylor, seem out of keeping with its announced spirit. The Festival management, with amateurish good will, lavished generosity on their friends.

• Producer Lou Adler was able to find a spot in the show for his own property, Johnny Rivers; Paul Simon for his friend, English folk singer Beverly; John Phillips for the Group Without A Name and Scott MacKenzie. None of them had the musical

Airplane high, but no new LP release

Jefferson Airplane has been taking more than a month to record their new album for RCA Victor. In a recording period of five weeks only five sides have been completed. No definite release date has been set.

Their usual recording schedule in Los Angeles begins at 11:00 p.m. in the evening and extends through six or seven in the morning. When they're not in the studios, they stay at a fabulous pink mansion which rents for $5,000 a month. The Beatles stayed at the house on their last American tour.

The house has two swimming pools and a variety of recreational facilities. It's a small small little paradise in the hills above Hollywood. Maybe suntans and guitars don't make it together.

status for an international pop music festival.

It is ironic that the Rivers and the rest appeared "free," but the money it cost the Festival to get them to Monterey and back, feed them, put them up (Beverly —*Continued on Page 7*

"THE WRITING OF THE BEATLES—or John and Paul's contribution to the Beatles in the late sixties—had a kind of depth to it, a more mature, more intellectual approach. We were different people, we were older. We knew each other all kinds of different ways than when we wrote together as teenagers and in our early twenties."

—JOHN

"WHEN WE DID *SGT. PEPPER*, we were just given a license to kill . . . so to speak, because we were already successful. And I knew that I could go in the studio and do just what I wanted, and I knew that they wanted to experiment a bit more. So we just let our hair down and went for broke."

—GEORGE MARTIN

The Beatles spent an unprecedented nine months producing *Sgt. Pepper's Lonely Hearts Club Band,* the first so-called rock concept album. When released in June 1967, it took the world by storm. Though the songs were often inspired by simple everyday things—"Being for the Benefit of Mr. Kite" came from a poster (*right*) in John's Kenwood home—the album was generally acclaimed as the pinnacle of rock's new sophistication. Its finale, John's powerful "A Day in the Life," was the album's most controversial track and its most musically ambitious. Symphony conductor and composer Leonard Bernstein wrote that the song "still sustained and rejuvenated me" fifteen years after he first heard the album.

W E WERE ALL ON THIS SHIP in the sixties, our generation, a ship going to discover the New World. And the Beatles were in the crow's nest of that ship. . . .

"We were part of it and contributed what we contributed; I can't designate what we did and didn't do. It depends on how each individual was impressed by the Beatles or how our shock wave went to different people. We were going through the changes, and all we were saying was, it's raining up here, or there's land or there's sun or we can see a seagull. We were just reporting what was happening to us."

—JOHN

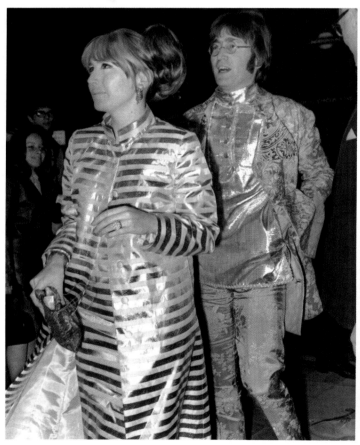

Previous page: During the late sixties the Beatles began to experiment in their music, and to assert their independence not only from the press's notions of how a Beatle should behave, but also from Brian's formatted style. Drugs began to play an increasingly important part in their lives. Cynthia (*above*) was concerned but said, "I couldn't switch John's brain off, could I?" *Right*: John at Weybridge.

I certainly earned a fortune as a Beatle . . . and spent a fortune. I mean, it was one big party!

JOHN

Above: John, Paul, Paul's girlfriend Jane Asher (*right*), Ringo and his wife Maureen (*left*) during the preview party for *Magical Mystery Tour,* which the Beatles wrote and produced. The BBC aired the film as a Christmas special on December 26, 1967. The critical drubbing it received proved that, artistically, the Beatles were something less than invincible. John and Julian (*right*) in front of the psychedelic Rolls.

M Y EARLIEST MEMORIES of my dad were between the ages of three and five, swimming in the pool with him, just doing kid stuff. He used to sit me on the front of his bike in front of him . . . and take me down to Ringo's once in a while, which was fun. I don't recall missing him when he went away on tours that much, because I was always preoccupied by my mother, school, and the fans at the gate, and whenever Dad came back, that was great. It was strange, but it didn't seem unusual because it was part of everyday life. . . .

"He had a gypsy caravan painted pretty much the same way as the psychedelic Rolls and had it put in a field down below the house in Weybridge, and it was just there for me and my pals, to mess around, like a little den or tree house, that kind of thing. We had fun messing around. . . . Growing up the son of a Beatle didn't seem any different to me as a kid. It was the people around me that made me notice that there was something different. It was hard to understand why people would like me more or dislike me for having a famous father. I didn't understand about the fame. It was difficult, but it was a learning thing."

—JULIAN LENNON

Julian (*above*) once brought home a drawing that he told his dad represented "Lucy in the sky with diamonds." John used the image in a song—then had to deny emphatically that the initials of the title stood for LSD. Everything the Beatles did during this period was scrutinized for its supposed hidden meaning. Weybridge (*left and overleaf*) was John's retreat from a hectic public life. But soon John and Cynthia began to drift apart. When the couple separated in 1968, Paul (*below*) visited Julian and started writing a song about him, which eventually became "Hey Jude."

"FOLLOWING A LECTURE that everybody had been to, to see the Maharishi, we were all invited to go to Bangor for a weekend to do meditation. And I, as usual, was trailing behind with the hand baggage . . . and a massive policeman put his arm out and stopped me, and I couldn't get on the train. The last thing that I saw was John's head peering out of the train window. And at that point I just felt, well, that's it, somehow. I can't explain it. Normally I wouldn't have broken down; I would have been pretty cool and calm, but at that point I just felt so sad, that this was symbolic of our life now. It's like 'I'm getting off at this station.' And it was pretty true after that. . . . When I finally did arrive in Bangor, that's when the terrible news came that Brian had died—that the door had to be kicked in, and that apparently he'd taken an overdose. We were so devastated. And at that point the panic set in, because Brian was the father figure. And all of a sudden that had finished."

—CYNTHIA

The six months from August 1967 to March 1968 were pivotal in John's life. George introduced the Beatles to the Maharishi Mahesh Yogi and to transcendental meditation; Brian Epstein died of an apparent drug overdose; the group found themselves in charge of the Beatle empire; and John began to correspond with Yoko Ono. *Above:* Cynthia at the train station in London; with John and the Maharishi in India (*right*).

IV

Enter Yoko

· · ·

I'm in love for the first time,
Don't you know it's going to last.
It's a love that lasts forever,
It's a love that has no past.

DON'T LET ME DOWN

Born in Tokyo, February 18, 1933—her father a wealthy Japanese banker, her mother from a princely merchant family— Yoko Ono (*below*) had a privileged but lonely childhood. She was raised in a cross-cultural environment and became well known as a performance artist in the New York avant-garde. In Cut Piece (*above*) Yoko sat on stage while members of the audience were invited to cut off bits of her clothing, piece by piece. At the age of twenty-five she married Toshi Ichiyanagi, one of Japan's foremost modern composers. After their divorce she married Tony Cox, and together they gained notoriety for their underground film *Bottoms,* which showed the derrieres of London's intelligentsia (*right*).

Yoko was having an art show in London at Indica Gallery, and I went down the night before the opening. The first thing that was in the gallery as you went in was a white stepladder and a painting on the ceiling and a spyglass hanging down. In those days most art put everybody down—got people upset. I walked up this ladder and picked up the spyglass. In teeny little writing it just said 'Yes.' And I made my decision to go and see the rest of the show. . . . If it had said 'No,' or something nasty like 'rip-off' or whatever, I would have left the gallery then. Because it said 'Yes' I thought, Okay, this is the first show I've been to that's said something warm to me."

—JOHN

"INITIALLY WHEN WE MET, I think there was a feeling of not really wanting to get together, because we knew—we knew this was a big one, both of us. . . . I thought he was very gentle, and then there was the moment where we just sort of looked at each other, especially when I gave him this card that said 'Breathe' and he did that really intently. And we started laughing—it was such a beautiful warm moment. And that's when I thought he was kind of great."

—YOKO ONO

I'D NEVER MET A WOMAN I considered as intelligent as me. That sounds bigheaded, but every woman I met was either a dolly-chick, or a sort of screwed-up intellectual chick. And of course, in the field I was in, I didn't meet many intelligent people anyway. And I always had this dream of meeting an artist, an artist girl who would be like me. And I thought it was a myth, but then I met Yoko and that was it."

—JOHN

"WE WERE FRIENDS, but also, we were partners. We inspired each other as independent artists, but also we were lovers. Well, I wasn't ready to have a relationship like that, and I'm sure that John was not expecting that at all either."

—YOKO

In 1967 John and Yoko began their artistic collaboration with Half a Wind show (*above*), where everyday objects were cut in half and painted white. The next year at the National Sculpture Exhibition they planted two acorns side by side on the grounds of Coventry Cathedral; Acorns for Peace (*left*) had a simple message: East meets West.

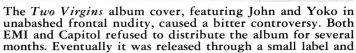

The *Two Virgins* album cover, featuring John and Yoko in unabashed frontal nudity, caused a bitter controversy. Both EMI and Capitol refused to distribute the album for several months. Eventually it was released through a small label and then only allowed in stores when it was repackaged in brown paper. Within a few months Cynthia filed for divorce from John, and Yoko began divorce proceedings against her second husband Tony Cox.

I HAD A KIND OF LITTLE STUDIO, which was really just a lot of tape recorders, and we made *Two Virgins* that way. She came over for a date, as it were, and I said, 'Do you want to go upstairs and play with the tapes?' So we did play with the tapes all night, and in the morning we made love as the sun came up. But we made this album's worth of sound together. We shot the cover ourselves, privately, and put out *Two Virgins,* and that started the whole shebang. . . . It was kind of a statement as well as an awakening for me, too. This is how I am really. This is me naked with the woman I love, so you want to share it? . . .

"It was only after we did it and started making the cover and seeing reactions from other Beatles and Apple staff, and we realized, 'My God, what a fuss this is creating.' But the more people that objected to it, the more we stuck to our guns. We realized there's something wrong here, if everybody was upset by the fact that two people were naked."
—JOHN

"I THINK WE SHARED our feelings with the world."
—YOKO

In late 1967 the Beatles launched the Apple organization as a record label and management company with a boutique at 94 Baker Street. Complaints by neighboring merchants forced the Beatles to paint over the building's mural (*left*). After seven months of losing money, the boutique closed as extravagantly as it had opened, by giving away its entire stock. *Above:* Yoko, John, and Paul in a rare photo of the three of them, taken at the premiere of *Yellow Submarine,* a full-length animated film that featured the Beatles as cartoon characters—and, in a brief singalong segment, as themselves.

INTERVIEWER: "What is Apple, John?"

Lennon: "It's a company we're setting up involving records, films, electronics, and manufacturing."

McCartney: "It's just trying to mix business with enjoyment. All the profits won't go into our pockets; it'll go to help people, but not like a charity."

Lennon: "Like if somebody wants to make a film and they get shown into the wastepaper bin. Nothing ever happens and they go around and they make an underground one and lots of people never see it. We hope to make a thing that's free, where people can just come and do and record and not have to ask, 'Can we have another mike in the studio, because we haven't had a hit yet?'"

—PRESS CONFERENCE

"I WAS TOO SCARED to break away from the Beatles, which I'd been looking to do since we stopped touring. And so I was sort of vaguely looking for somewhere to go but didn't have the nerve to really step out into the boat by myself, so I sort of hung around, and when I met Yoko and fell in love, my God, this is different than anything before. This is more than a hit record. It's more than gold. It's more than everything. . . . When I met Yoko is when you meet your first woman, and you leave the guys at the bar, and you don't go play football anymore. Once I found the woman, the boys became of no interest whatsoever, other than they were like old school friends. Y'know that song: 'Those wedding bells are breaking up that old gang of mine. . . .'"

—JOHN

"ONE NIGHT I went to bed with this guy and suddenly the next morning I see these three guys standing there with resentful eyes—you know, three relatives standing around staring at me."

—YOKO

129

On October 18, 1968, police raided Ringo's Montague Square apartment, where John and Yoko were living. Charged with possession of marijuana and obstructing police, John wound up pleading guilty to possession *(above)*.

Anybody who knows our history knows that we went through all hell together—through miscarriages and terrible times.

JOHN

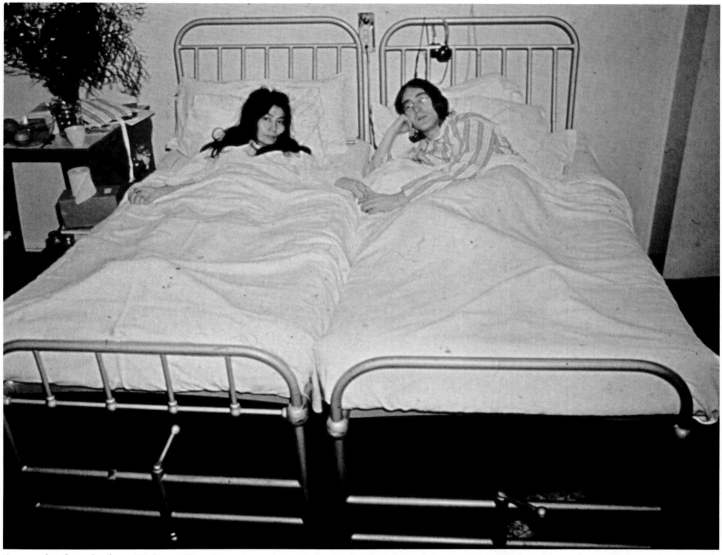

A month after the bust Yoko suffered a miscarriage. John had a bed set up in the hospital, so he could be at her side. The ba- by's heartbeat was recorded and later became part of their 1969 album, *Unfinished Music No. 2 —Life with the Lions.*

On December 11, 1968, John and Yoko (*above*) participated in the Rock and Roll Circus, a Rolling Stones film project. Because of legal and artistic problems, the movie was never released. *Right:* John performs with Eric Clapton, Mitch Mitchell, and Keith Richards. It was the first time since the early days that John had performed without the Beatles, and he was exhilarated. "It was great to have a different noise coming out behind me. . . . I thought, Wow! It's fun with other people."

Above: John, Julian, and Yoko with friend Brian Jones of the Rolling Stones. Months later Brian drowned in his pool at age twenty-five, an apparent drug victim. His death and, within a relatively short time, those of Janis Joplin and Jimi Hendrix left John shaken. *Overleaf:* Yoko sat in with the Beatles at Twickenham Film Studios during the recording sessions for *Let It Be*. The Beatles hired director Michael Lindsay-Hogg to film the sessions to fulfill a feature film commitment.

I THINK THE BASIC THING nobody asks is why do people take drugs of any sort? And that question has to be resolved before you can think, well, what can we do for the poor drug addict? Why do we have to have these accessories to normal living to live? I mean, is there something wrong with society that's making us so pressurized, that we cannot live without guarding ourselves against it? . . .

"Once you're so depressed that you get into drugs, once you're on them, it's very, very hard to see the light or to have any kind of hope. All you think about is the drug, and it's no good us preaching at people and saying don't take them. Because that doesn't work. It's like the church telling you not to drink or not to have sex when you're a kid. There's nothing on earth gonna do it. But if people take any notice of what we say, we say we've been through the drug scene, man, and there's nothing like being straight. You need hope, and hope is something that you build up within yourself and with your friends. It's a very difficult situation, drugs. . . . The worst drugs are as bad as anybody's told you. It's just a dumb trip, which I can't condemn people if they get into it, because one gets into it for one's own personal, social, emotional reasons. It's something to be avoided if one can help it."
—JOHN

The Beatles performed in public for the last time on January 30, 1969. The famous concert atop the Apple Building at 3 Saville Row (*left*) was the conclusion of the movie *Let It Be*. After five songs were performed, Lennon said, "I'd like to say thank you on behalf of the group and ourselves, and I hope we passed the audition." *Above:* With the Beatles are the women often accused of breaking up the group: Linda Eastman, who married Paul in March of that year, and Yoko.

WHEN JOHN HITCHED UP with Yoko, he said Yoko is now a part of me. As I have a right and left hand, so I have Yoko, that's me. Wherever I am, she is. And it was a bit difficult to deal with. It was an irritation for me. Suddenly she would appear in the control room, nobody would say anything to me. . . . I wasn't even introduced to her, but she would just sit there, and her influence would be felt. And so, consequently, to begin with, everyone was irritated by it. Even when she was ill, her bed was brought into the studio so she could be present while they were recording. It was rather bizarre."

—GEORGE MARTIN

"I'M INTERESTED IN John's work and my work, and in the work that we do together. But I'm not that interested in the Beatles because, well, that's something else. Most of the time conversations tend to be about Beatles. I don't realize that usually. But when I do, it's a strange feeling, really."

—YOKO

"IT'S NOT THAT THE BEATLES didn't like each other. I've compared it to a marriage. It was a long relationship. It started many, many years before the American public or the English public, for that matter, knew us. Paul and I were together since he was fifteen, I was sixteen, and George was fourteen. The four of us had been together for a long, long time. Epstein was dead and people were bothering us with business. The whole pressure of it finally got to us. And we mainly took it out on each other. It finally became apparent that we were trying to create something phony. . . . By the time we got to *Let It Be* we couldn't play the game anymore. We could see through each other and therefore we felt uncomfortable. Because up until then we really believed intensely in what we were doing, and the product we put out and everything had to be just right, and . . . we believed. Suddenly we didn't believe. It came to a point where it was no longer creating magic, and the camera being in the room with us made us aware of that. That we'd come to a stage where we would be completely phony—no reality left. And that was the end of it."

—JOHN

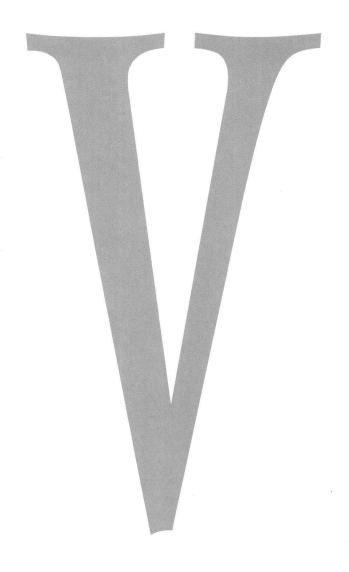

V

1969

· · ·

Talking in our beds for a week
The news people said,
"Say, whatcha doin' in bed?"
I said, "We're only tryin' to get
us some peace."

THE BALLAD OF JOHN AND YOKO

I N 'LUCY IN THE SKY WITH DIAMONDS' I was visualizing *Alice in Wonderland,* an image of this female who would come and save me—a girl with kaleidoscope eyes who would be the real love of my life. Lucy turned out to be Yoko. . . .

"With us it's a teacher-pupil relationship. That's what people don't understand. She's the teacher and I'm the pupil. I'm the famous one. I'm supposed to know everything. But she taught me everything I fucking know. . . .

"We've broken down a few barriers between us, which we had to do because we had two big egos, two individual artists—and with love we overcame that.

"We've got this gift of love, but love is like a precious plant. You can't just accept it and leave it in the cupboard or just think it's going to get on by itself. You've got to keep watering it. You've got to really look after it and nurture it. . . .

"Before Yoko and I met, we were half a person. You know there's an old myth about people being half and the other half being in the sky, or in heaven or on the other side of the universe or a mirror image. But we are two halves, and together we're a whole."

—JOHN

By 1969 John had turned much of his creative energies toward working with Yoko. They formed the Plastic Ono Band, a constantly changing group, of which they were the only permanent members. The idea was to free John from the confines of the carefully produced Beatles albums.

145

Yoko and John, holding their wedding license (*left*), married in Gibraltar on March 20, 1969. They interrupted their honeymoon in Paris (*above*) to stage their first bed-in for peace at the Amsterdam Hilton. The news media in general treated the event cynically, and in Britain the papers called the couple "Joko." But as John said, "Yoko and I knew that whatever we did was going to be in the papers, so we decided to utilize the space by getting married with a commercial for peace." Two months later they held another bed-in in Montreal, where they recorded "Give Peace a Chance." Although later the Plastic Ono Band was given performing credit, John still listed the songwriters as Lennon/McCartney.

Rituals are important. Nowadays it's hip not to be married. I'm not interested in being hip.

JOHN

John began work in 1969 on a series of lithographs called Bag One, which were later displayed at the London Arts Gallery. The works created a huge furor, and eight of the prints, including this drawing of Yoko (*left*), were confiscated by authorities who claimed they were obscene. *Above:* John's sketch of his and Yoko's wedding. *Overleaf right:* The lithograph series was introduced by this whimsical alphabet. *Overleaf left:*

In April 1969 they demonstrated the concept of Bagism to British TV talk-show host Eamonn Andrews, inviting him to join them in an impromptu "bed-in." By concealing themselves in a bag, John and Yoko set out to show the importance of ideas over appearances. *Following pages:* On the Apple building rooftop that spring John formally changed his name to John Ono Lennon.

As a Beatle, I'd made it, and there was nothing to do. We had money, we had fame, and there was no joy. Then I met Yoko, and she was making it as an avant-garde artist, and we both tried to find something we had in common. A common goal in life, because she couldn't rock with me, and I couldn't avant-garde with her—that's what we thought at the time. So we decided the thing we had in common was love. And from love came peace, so we decided to work for world peace.

". . . We crossed over into each other's fields, like people do from country to pop. We did it from avant-garde left field to pop left field. We tried to find a ground that was interesting to both of us. And we both got excited and stimulated by each other's experiences. . . .

"We're all in a bag, you know? . . . I was in a pop bag, going round and round, in my little clique. And she was in her little avant-garde clique, going round and round. . . . So we just came up with a word. If you'd ask us what Bagism is, we'd say, 'We're all in a bag, baby.'"

—JOHN

"EVERYBODY'S AN ARTIST. Everybody's God, you know. It's just that they're inhibited. I believe in people so much that if the whole of civilization is burned so we don't have any memory of it, even then people will start to build their own art. It is a necessity—a function. We don't need history."

—YOKO

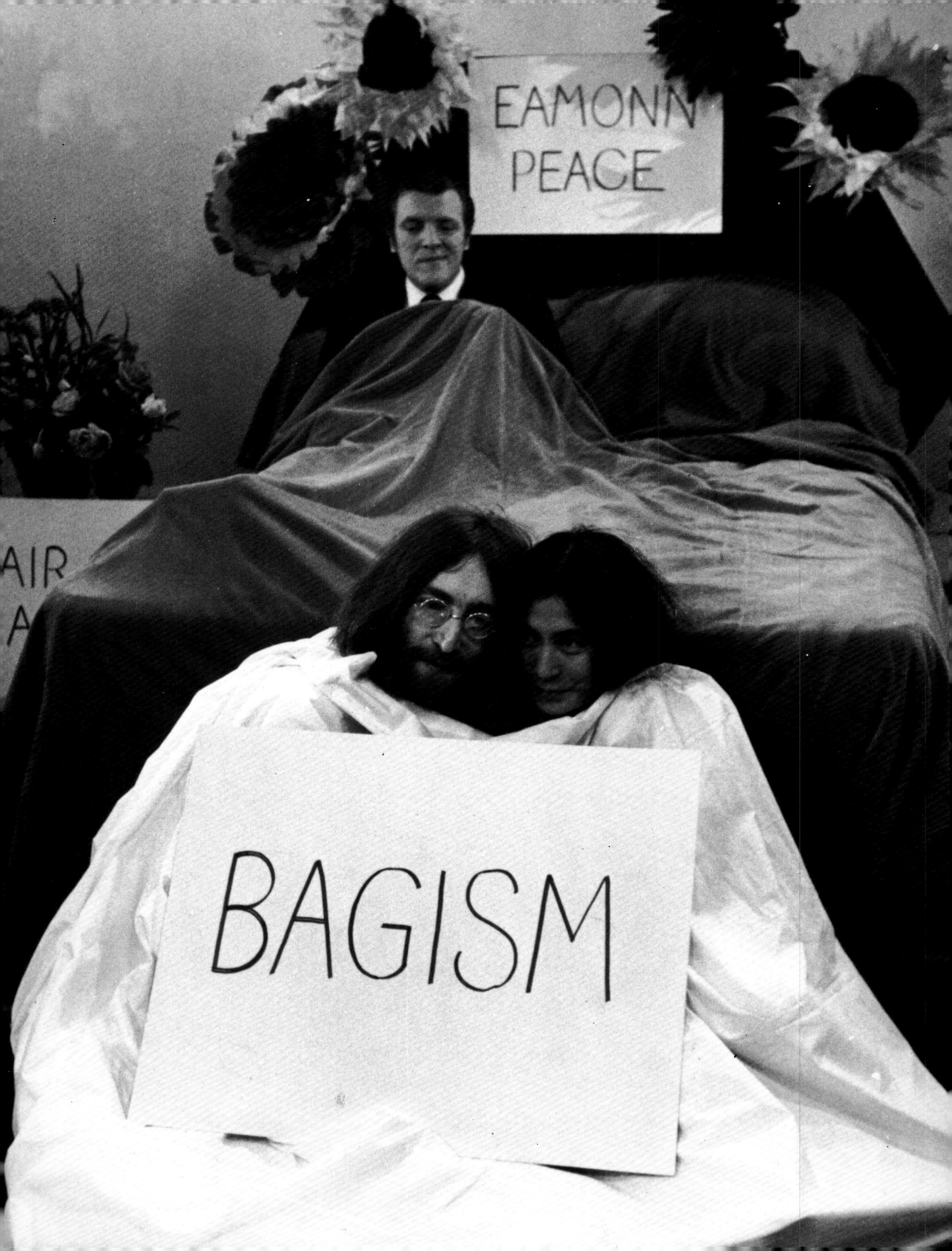
EAMONN
PEACE
AIR
A
BAGISM

A is for Parrot which we can plainly see.
B is for glasses which we can plainly see.
C is for plastic which we can plainly see
D is for Doris
E is for binoculars I'll get it in five
F is for Ethel who lives next door
G is for Orange which we love to eat when we can get them because
they come from abroad.
H is for England and (Heather)
I is for monkey we see in the tree
J is for parrot which we can plainly see.
K is for shoetop we wear to the ball
L is for lamo because brum
M is for Venezuela where the oranges come from
N is for Brazil near Venezuela (very near)
O is for football which we kick about a bit
T is for Tommy who won the war
Q is a garden which we can plainly see
R is for intestines which hurt when we dance
S is for pancake or whole wheat bread.
U is for Ethel who lives on the hill
P is arab and her sister will
V is for we
W is for lighter which never lights
X is easter — have one yourself
Y is a crooked letter and you can't straighten it
Z is for Apple which we can plainly see.

This is my story both humble and true
take it to pieces and mend it with glue.

John Lennon 1969. Feb.

Left: In July 1969 John took Julian, Yoko, and her daughter Kyoko to visit his relatives in Scotland. On the return trip their car overturned, and they suffered minor injuries. *Above:* John and Yoko on their release from the hospital. Two years later they became embroiled in a custody battle with Kyoko's father Tony Cox. When Yoko finally won custody, Cox disappeared with the child and, despite an intense search, Yoko never reunited with her daughter.

Y OU CAN'T CHEAT KIDS. If you cheat them when they're children they'll make you pay when they're sixteen or seventeen by revolting against you or hating you or all those so-called teenage problems. I think that's finally when they're old enough to stand up to you and say, 'What a hypocrite you've been all this time. You've never given me what I really wanted, which is you.'"

—JOHN

"I WAS AN OFFBEAT MOTHER from the beginning. I wasn't always with her, though there was spiritual communication between us. But since she disappeared there was a time in my life when John and I would be watching TV and a child would come on the screen . . . we would switch the channel because I couldn't bear seeing children. Because it reminded me of Kyoko."

—YOKO

In September John and Yoko appeared at the Toronto Rock 'n' Roll Revival as the Plastic Ono Band with Eric Clapton, Klaus Voormann, and Alan White. In December they returned to announce plans for a 1970 peace-and-music festival. *Above:* Outside Toronto, at singer Ronnie Hawkins's farmhouse, where they set up temporary headquarters.

Denied entry into the United States because of John's drug bust, the couple staged a high-profile bed-in at the Queen Elizabeth Hotel in Montreal from which they broadcast their message for peace to America.

Later in December John and Yoko, with a small entourage, took a glass-enclosed train car (*above*) to Ottawa for a private meeting with Canadian Prime Minister Pierre Trudeau, who had expressed a desire to see Lennon. Following their meeting John said, "If there were more leaders like Mr. Trudeau, the world would have peace."

I F BEING AN EGOMANIAC means I believe in what I do and in my art or my music, then in that respect you can call me that. . . . I believe in what I do, and I'll say it. . . .

"People want peace. And you've got to sell it and sell it and sell it. So we do the bed-ins and they say, 'What? They're in bed? What's this?' And all we're doing really is donating our holiday. We get tired and it's . . . more convenient for us to stay in one spot than to go around doing press conferences."

—JOHN

"I FEEL THAT BOTH OF US are actually doing things to change the world . . . for the better. We don't go to Trafalgar Square to sit or march. We don't believe that's the only way. Our way may be quieter and slower. People may think that we're just avoiding problems and hassles, but it's not like that at all. Actually, John's songs, the vibration he's sending to the world through his songs, and the things that we're doing together, are all changing the world, I think."

—YOKO

"NOW, IN THE SIXTIES we were naive, like children. Everybody went back to their rooms, and said, 'We didn't get a wonderful world of just flowers and peace and happy chocolate, and it won't be just pretty and beautiful all the time,' and just like babies everyone went back to their rooms and sulked. 'We're going to stay in our rooms and play rock and roll and not do anything else, because the world's a horrible place, because it didn't give us everything we cried for.' Right?

"Well, crying for it wasn't enough. The thing the sixties did was to show us the possibilities and the responsibility that we all had. It wasn't the answer. It just gave us a glimpse of the possibility."

—JOHN

Beginning on December 15, 1969, John and Yoko launched their far-reaching War Is Over campaign with posters and billboards in a dozen cities around the world (*left and below*).

With political activist Michael X (*above*), John and Yoko donate hair they cut off, for an auction to raise money for the Black House, a center for black culture in London.

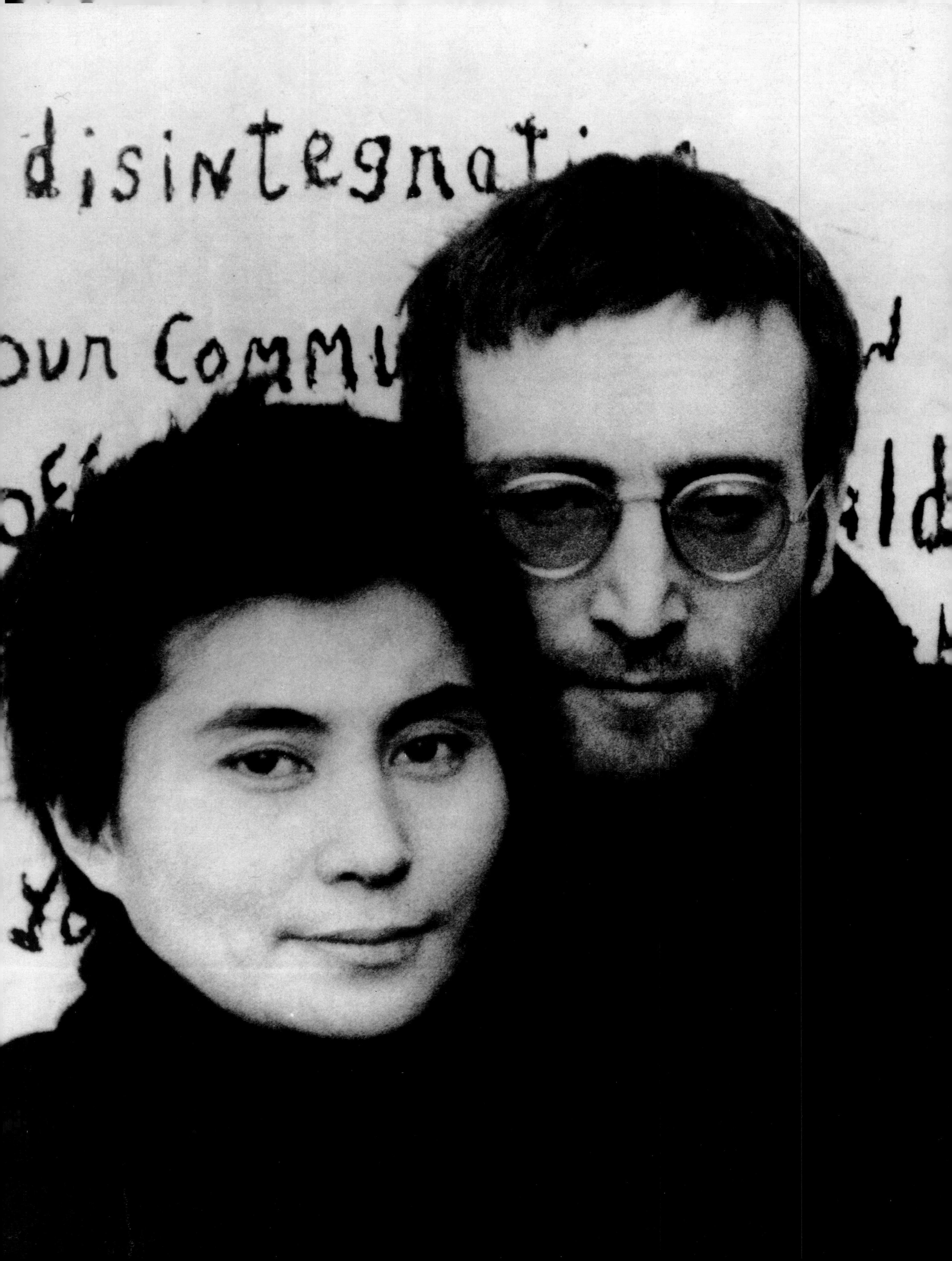
disintegrat
our Commu

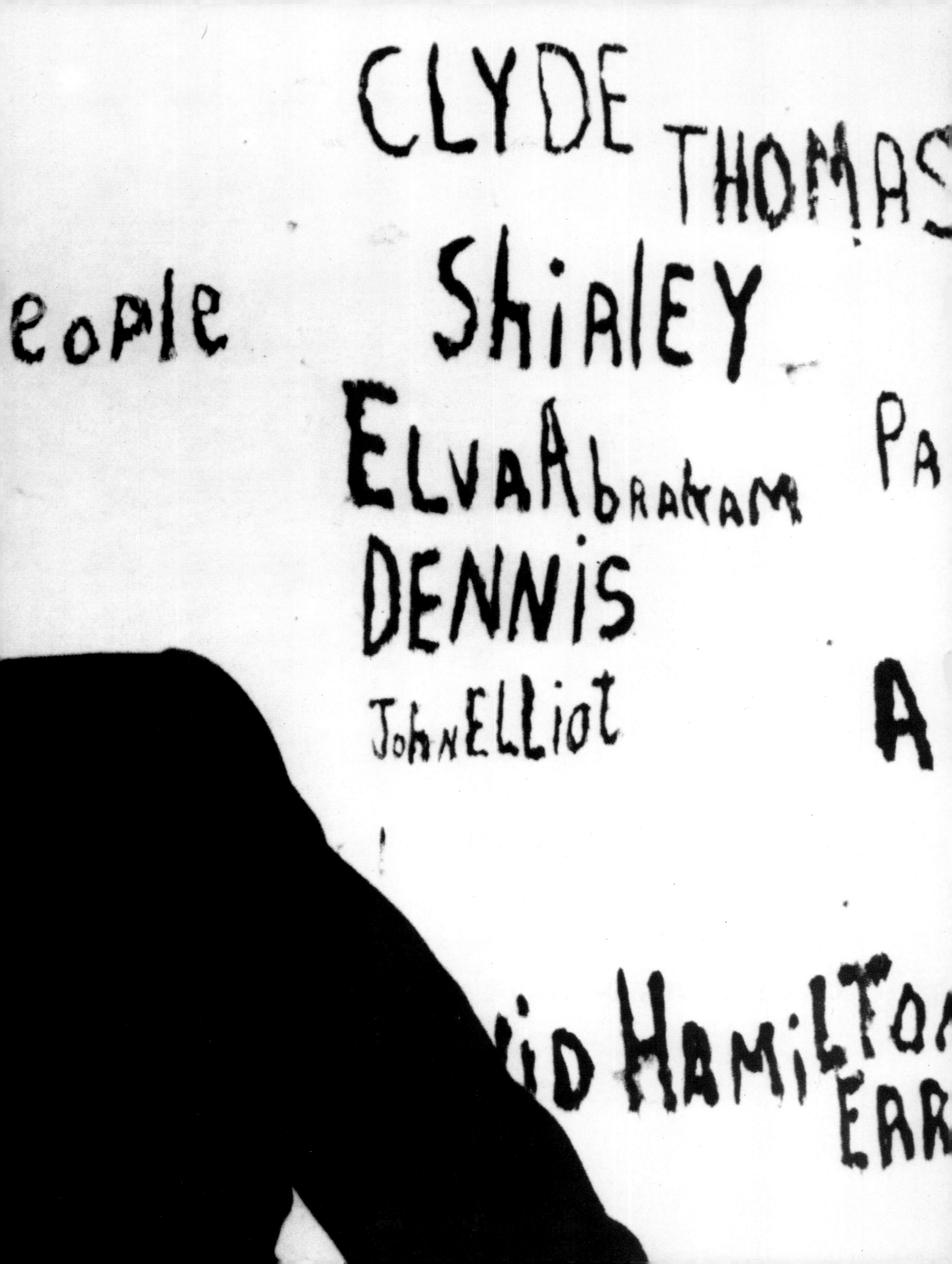

CLYDE THOMAS

eople

Shirley

ElvaAbraham Pa

DENNIS

A

JohnELLiot

!

id HamilTon

ERR

VI

The Dream Is Over

· · ·

The dream is over, yesterday
I was the dream weaver, but now I'm reborn.
I was the walrus, but now I'm John,
And so, dear friends, you'll just have to carry on.

GOD

Weel haven't been apart for more than one hour in two years. Everything we do is together, and that's what gives us our strength.

JOHN

In May 1969 John and Yoko bought Tittenhurst Park, an eighteenth-century Georgian mansion on a seventy-acre estate in Ascot. Only twenty-six miles from London, it offered a tranquil retreat during one of their most hectic and productive periods. There John and Yoko built an eight-track recording studio, where Phil Spector and George Harrison, among others, came to help John record the album *Imagine*.

W**HEN I THINK OF ASCOT** I think of making *Imagine* and also just being together, strolling around in the gardens. We together declared to the world that we were a working partnership. It was a very intense and beautiful time for us."

—YOKO

"I BELIEVE IN EVERYTHING until it's disproved. So I believe in fairies, the myths, dragons. It all exists, even if it's in your mind. Who's to say that dreams and nightmares aren't as real as the here and now? Reality leaves a lot to the imagination."

—JOHN

At Tittenhurst (*right*) John read *The Primal Scream* by Arthur Janov, a California psychiatrist who had his patients confront their earliest and deepest emotions by screaming away the pain. Impressed with Janov's theories, John and Yoko invited him to Ascot, where they began primal therapy sessions. "I went to Janov to learn to cry," John later said.

Though John wrote the lyrics to "Imagine" on the back of a hotel bill while flying in an airplane, he composed the music at Tittenhurst. It was here that most of the songs for this, his masterpiece album, were written. *Imagine* combined the cre- ative genius that had marked his Beatles work with the powerful political and social messages that defined his later songs, and left no doubt that for John there was definitely life after the Beatles.

S ONGWRITING IS about getting the demon out of me. It's like being possessed. You try to go to sleep, but the song won't let you. So you have to get up and make it into something, and then you're allowed to sleep. It's always in the middle of the bloody night, or when you're half-awake or tired, when your critical faculties are switched off. So letting go is what the whole game is. Every time you try to put your finger on it, it slips away. You turn on the lights and the cockroaches run away. You can never grasp them. . . .

"Everything I've ever done is out. I don't have boxes of unreleased stuff. There's nothing in the files. I never keep anything unless I don't like the sound of it or it didn't work. If I can sing it to an engineer, I can sing it to anyone. . . .

"I still don't know how to express the really delicate personal stuff. People think that *Plastic Ono* is very personal, but there are some subtleties of emotions which I cannot seem to express in pop music, and it frustrates me. Maybe that's why I still search for other ways of expressing myself. Songwriting is a limiting experience in some ways— writing down words that have to rhyme."

—JOHN

Imagine' crystallized John's dream. It crystallized his idealism. It was something he really wanted to say to the world.

YOKO

Phil Spector produced *Imagine* with John and sang backup vocals (*top*). George Harrison (*above*) played on several songs, including "How Do You Sleep?" an angry response to Paul's apparent jabs at John and Yoko in his solo album, *Ram*. *Imagine*'s recording sessions were filmed for a TV documentary (*left*).

IN BRITAIN I'M THE GUY who got lucky and won the pools, and Yoko's the Hawaiian who married the guy who got lucky and won the pools. In America we're artists. . . .

"I've met a lot of New Yorkers who complain about it, but nobody moves out. New York is what Paris was in the twenties . . . the center of the art world. And we want to be in the center. It's the greatest place on earth.

"I love the place 'cause this is where the music came from, this is what influenced my whole life and got me where I am today. . . . I've got a lot of friends here and I even brought my own cash."

—JOHN

"BOTH OF US had a lot of feelings about this city. John often said that if he were born in New York, then he would have been very hip from the beginning. I always thought it was a very funny statement, because he was hip anyway. But that's how he felt. . . .

"The thing he discovered while we were living in New York is that he'd see the resemblance to Liverpool—the docks, the piers, you know. And he said this is like going back to Liverpool. It's a big Liverpool. And the taxi drivers talking—not in a Liverpool accent—but with a rough edge. So maybe that's what he was drawn to subconsciously."

—YOKO

In early 1972, shortly after the release of *Imagine*, John and Yoko moved to New York City (*right*) and began efforts to gain permanent residency. John was tired of the red tape every visit to the United States entailed. His 1968 drug bust was cited as the main reason he was denied a visa, but John and Yoko believed they were being persecuted for their political statements.

I've had the boyhood thing of being Elvis. Now I want to be with my best friend, and my best friend's my wife. Who could ask for anything more?

JOHN

One of the things about New York that most amazed John and Yoko was the way they could move about the city (*above*) without being overwhelmed by fans. They first rented a two-room apartment on Bank Street in Greenwich Village (*right*). Later they moved into the elegant Dakota Apartments overlooking Central Park.

In New York John and Yoko formed alliances with the American left, including 1960s radicals Jerry Rubin and Abbie Hoffman. *Above:* They appeared at an antiwar demonstration in Central Park in April 1972 and also produced an album for Greenwich Village musician David Peel that was banned worldwide because of the song "The Pope Smokes Dope."

I THINK OUR SOCIETY is run by insane people for insane objectives. And I think that's what I expressed when I was sixteen, and twelve, all the way down the line. . . . I think we're being run by maniacs for maniacal ends . . . and I think I'm liable to be put away as insane for expressing that. That's what's insane about it. . . .

"If it gets to destruction, you can count me out. But I'm not sure, you know, I'm human, and I'm liable to change depending on the situation, but I prefer nonviolence. . . .

"We've been on our peace gig, as we call it, for a year solid. And people say, 'Do you think it's having any effect?' I can't answer that. It's like asking me in the Cavern, 'Are you gonna make it?' In the back of my mind I thought, I'm gonna make it, but I couldn't lay it on the line. And I think that peace is more tangible than Beatles."

—JOHN

"I KNOW THAT IF I LEFT, I'd have a hell of a job getting back in. I mean I was having a hell of a job coming in and out as it was. So does Paul, so does Mick [Jagger], so does George. When they want to come in, they have to get on their knees six months in advance. And I got sick of that. So, I wanted to stay. . . .

"They're even changing their own rules to get us, just 'cause we're peaceniks really. . . . Let's just say that a few friends of ours in the pop business that have exactly the same [marijuana] conviction as me are allowed to come and go as they like. They just don't have the same point of view as me, or they don't state it. . . .

"When it first started, I was followed in a car, and my phone was tapped. . . . And I think they wanted to scare me, and I was scared—paranoid. And people thought I was crazy. 'Lennon, you bigheaded maniac. Who's going to follow you around? What do they want?' That's what I want to know. What do they want? I'm not going to cause them any problem."

—JOHN

Convinced that Lennon was going to disrupt the Republican National Convention, the United States government tried to deport him in 1972. John and Yoko took their case to the peo- ple through the press (*above*). Recently revealed documents show that the FBI had monitored their lives. *Overleaf:* John and Yoko began to feel these outside pressures on their marriage.

Nothing will stop me, and whether I'm here or wherever I may be, I'll always have the same feelings [and] I'll say what I feel.

JOHN

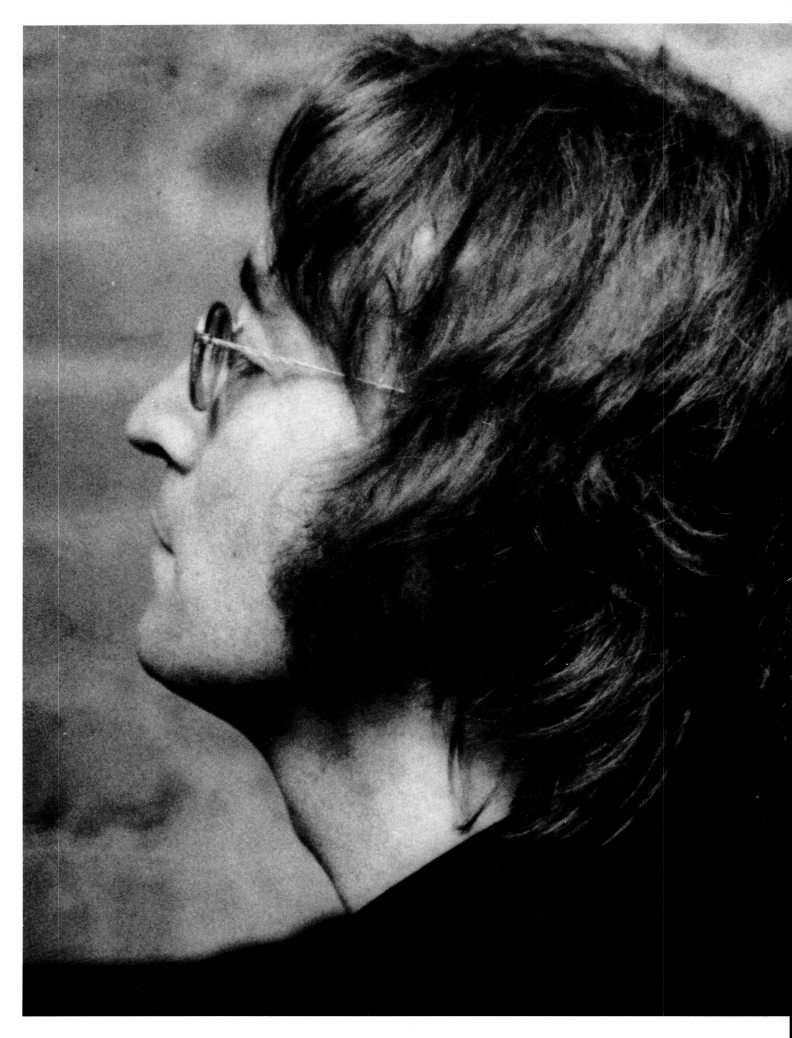

John and Yoko separated for eighteen months, a period that John termed his "lost weekend," when he drank heavily, indulging what he called his "self-destructive" side. He spent much of this time at the Los Angeles home (*left*) of his friend Elliot Mintz, but his constant companion was May Pang, who had worked for John and Yoko as a personal assistant. In New York and Los Angeles they hung out with such rock and roll stars as Mick Jagger (*overleaf*), and John joined Bette Midler and Atlantic Records chief Ahmet Ertegun (*above*) at a music industry awards ceremony.

BY THEN IT WAS GETTING OBVIOUS to even the most unworldly couple that the world didn't really want us to work together. John wanted to insist on it. It was not only bad, it seemed, for John's career but in a way I lost my career. I mean, I could do something as Mrs. Lennon, but I really lost my identity as Yoko Ono. . . . I said to John we're both still young, and we have a beautiful future. Why kill it by trying to be together? Let's give ourselves a chance and see what happens. . . .

"I said, 'Look, why don't you just go to L.A. and have fun. And leave me alone.' I just wanted to think straight because I couldn't think straight anymore."

—YOKO

"SHE LITERALLY SAID, 'Get out!' And I thought, Okay, okay, I'm going! I hadn't been a bachelor since I was twenty or something, so at first I thought, Whoopee! . . .

"When you're thirty-five, you can't take as much booze . . . and I always got a little violent on drink. . . . So it was a kind of self-destructive suicide side of me, which is resolving itself for the better, I believe, because I never enjoyed it. . . .

"At first I thought, Oh, bachelor life! And then I woke up one day and thought, What is this? I want to go home. But Yoko wouldn't let me home. That's why it was eighteen months instead of six. Because we were talking all the time on the phone and I kept saying, 'I don't like this, I'm out of control, I'm drinking, and I'm getting into trouble, and I'd like to come home.' She's saying, 'You're not ready to come home.' Okay, back to the bottle. . . ."

—JOHN

Between late 1973 and early 1975, despite the separation, John remained prolific. His creative output included three albums: *Mind Games, Walls and Bridges,* and *Rock 'n' Roll.* He also produced Harry Nilsson's *Pussycats* album at the Record Plant in Los Angeles (*above*). *Right:* Creativity, however, did not preclude drinking bouts. In March 1974 he was roughly ejected from Los Angeles's Troubadour club after heckling the Smothers Brothers comedy team.

THE LOST WEEKEND was a combination of a remarkable party, an exercise into the depths of foolishness, and I think John's last effort to assert his manhood. It was his departure from his youth, to becoming a man, to wanting to be with Yoko, to having a child. Some people have bachelor parties, John had a lost weekend.

"The worst thing I can say about John was that he was an absolutely miserable drunk. Two brandy alexanders and he was charming, delightful, told the old stories, was witty and lovely. By the third he started to snarl, and after that he was uncontrollable."

—ELLIOT MINTZ

"THEY GOT MAD AT ME for not saying 'Peace, brother' all the time. I'm human. I wasn't having any peace myself, so I couldn't be going around saying 'Peace, brother.' Am I supposed to go around like a nun? . . .

"I can't do it. I couldn't do it in the Beatles and I can't do it by myself. . . . I have to cut through, cut through the mask even if it's self-created.

"Yoko was the only one who didn't put me down for that period, because a) she knew I was suffering, and b) she said, 'You didn't kill anyone. You didn't abuse anyone.' And I thought, Okay, okay, she doesn't mind it, so I'm not going to give a damn whether the reporter likes it or not."

—JOHN

The worst was being separated from Yoko and realizing that I literally could not survive without her.

JOHN

When Elton John agreed to play keyboards on John Lennon's single "Whatever Gets You thru the Night," he wagered that the song would reach number one on the charts. A doubtful Lennon promised that if it did, he would perform at one of Elton's shows. Elton won the bet, and on November 28, 1974, John appeared at Elton's Madison Square Garden concert. Yoko, who was in the audience, met John backstage. "We were sitting there just looking at each other and that was it," she later said.

By early 1975 John and Yoko had reconciled, and Yoko was pregnant when they appeared with David Bowie, Art Garfunkel, and Paul Simon at the Grammy Awards ceremony (*above*).

John's last public performance (*right*) was for a British televised tribute to Sir Lew Grade, an important record industry figure, in June.

WE WERE SEPARATED for eighteen months. The Beatles didn't get back together again, did they? So it was not Yoko who kept them apart. I did see Paul in Los Angeles. And I saw a lot of Ringo. The only one I didn't see was George. . . .

"When [Yoko and I] got back together, we decided that this was our life. That having a baby was important to us, and that everything else was subsidiary to that, and therefore everything else had to be abandoned. I mean, abandonment gave us the fulfillment we were looking for and the space to breathe. . . ."

—JOHN

"WHEN YOKO FINALLY SAID it was okay for him to come home, there was this tremendous sigh of relief. It was a reinstatement of his own manhood—that he was worthy of her. Because if he wasn't worthy of Yoko, he was only going to be worthy of having fleeting, meaningless relationships with women who said the right things to guys who used to be Beatles. And that terrified him."

—ELLIOT MINTZ

As John continued to fight for permanent residency in the United States, he flashed the peace sign in front of the Statue of Liberty (*left*). Finally, in July 1976, as the nation celebrated its Bicentennial, John won his green card (*above*) from the U.S. Department of Immigration. With John's residency status assured, he and Yoko settled into life at the Dakota.

VII

Househusband

· · ·

When I say that I'm okay,
They look at me kind of strange
Surely you're not happy now,
You no longer play the game.

WATCHING THE WHEELS

T HE PROGNOSIS WAS, 'She's too old.' She was forty-three, so they said, 'No way.' She's had too many miscarriages. But that's when I really realized that I *did* want a child. I wanted *Yoko's* baby. Not just *a* baby. We worked hard for that child. So this is what they call a love child in truth. . . .

"The joy is still there when I see Sean. He didn't come out of my belly, but my God, I've made his bones, because I've attended to every meal, and how he sleeps, and the fact that he swims like a fish because I took him to the ocean. I'm so proud of all those things. But he is my biggest pride."

—JOHN

Sean Taro Ono Lennon was born on October 9, 1975. During the next five years John turned all his attention to raising Sean, overseeing every detail. He felt that cribs were wooden cages for children, so Sean slept between his parents throughout much of his infancy.

The most important thing in my father's life? World peace. Me and my brother. My mom.

SEAN

Julian, who lived with his mother in North Wales, England, often visited John, as they began to develop a deeper relationship. During this time John was also able to make peace with his own father, shortly before Alfred Lennon's death. As he said, "Everybody has their problems, including wayward fathers." *Overleaf:* Sean's fourth birthday and John's thirty-ninth were celebrated at the Tavern on the Green, a restaurant in Central Park.

THE THING THAT I REMEMBER most about my father was watching 'The Muppet Show' and 'Dr. Jekyll and Mr. Hyde' at bedtime. First we'd watch 'Dr. Jekyll and Mr. Hyde,' then 'The Muppet Show' because I was scared, so I'd have to, you know, cool down. Then we'd wrestle, and then I'd be asleep by the end of wrestling, so he'd carry me into my room and in the hallway he would say stuff like 'Well, Sean, what did we do today?' and we'd talk about what we did in the day, and then he would put me in this little bunk bed. I was really small, though, so I could fit. And there was a little mobile of these planes over my bed, and my ceiling was painted like a sky, so I thought the planes were flying in the sky. And then he'd say, 'Good night, Sean,' and he'd turn the lights on and off to his voice. I thought that was the greatest magic trick in the world."

—SEAN

"THE LAST YEAR, I would say, was the best. I was growing older, I began to understand things a lot more and understand Dad, too. It was at a point where we could call each other and say, 'Would you like to come over?' There was no wall facing us anymore. There was always something between us, but it had been knocked down, and I could say, 'Hi, Dad, I'd like to come and see you, is that okay?' 'Yeah.' Towards the end we were definitely getting closer and closer."

—JULIAN

While John was becoming a househusband, Yoko was becoming the family's financial manager. She achieved substantial success, often seeking counsel from psychics and numerologists. Yoko's investments—all ecologically sound—included dairy farms, artworks, and properties such as the yacht *Isis* (*above*) and a $700,000 beachfront mansion, El Salano (*right*) in West Palm Beach, Florida.

In the late seventies John and Yoko, who previously had documented so much of their relationship on film, shot only a handful of home movies and took Polaroid photos. Elliot Mintz, who saw a lot of John, described this period as one of "personal discovery and revelation" for John. "He recharged his batteries and reexamined his priorities."

I don't buy that bit about quality [time] over quantity [time]—that an hour a week of intense rolling around together is better than twenty minutes every day of just being yourself around him. . . .

JOHN

John and Yoko frequently went to Japan for family vacations, which gave them the opportunity to familiarize Sean with his Japanese heritage. These photographs (*here, overleaf, and the following six pages*) were taken by Japanese photographer Nishi Fumiya Saimaru, who worked for John and Yoko as a personal assistant and traveled with them to the Far East.

Though Yoko was tied to New York because of business obligations, John traveled often—to Cairo, Capetown, Hong Kong, and Singapore—sometimes alone, sometimes with family. *Above:* With Sean at a temple in Hong Kong.

THE PRESSURES of being a parent are equal to any pressure on earth. To be a conscious parent, and really look to that little being's mental and physical health is a responsibility which most of us, including me, avoid most of the time, because it's too hard. . . . To put it loosely, the reason why kids are crazy is because nobody can face the responsibility of bringing them up. . . .

"If [Sean] doesn't see me a few days or if I'm really, really busy, and I just sort of get a glimpse of him, or if I'm feeling depressed without him even seeing me, he sort of picks up on it. And he starts getting that way. So I can no longer afford to have artistic depressions. If I start wallowing in a depression, he'll start coming down with stuff, so I'm sort of obligated to keep up. And sometimes I can't, because something will make me depressed and sure as hell he'll get a cold or trap his finger in a door or something, and so now I have sort of more reason to stay healthy and bright. . . .

"I think it's better for him to see me as I am. If I'm grumpy, I'm grumpy. If I'm not, I'm not. So if I want to play, I'll play. If I don't, I don't. I don't kowtow to him. I'm as straight with him as I can be. . . . I'm just hoping that whatever I give now, which is time, I won't have to pay later."

—JOHN

"THE FACT that my father almost completely stopped his musical career to raise me makes me feel good. I never really registered that he was a Beatle until I saw a movie called *Yellow Submarine,* and I just put it together, and I would ask about it, and he would say, 'Yeah, I was a Beatle, but that's over now, and I'm spending time with you.' I think it's great that he would take time out for five years to raise me. He said the first five years of a child's life are the most important, and I guess they are, you know."

—SEAN

While in Japan John immersed himself in the culture and, with Yoko and Sean, would often visit Buddhist temples, where they prayed and meditated. *Overleaf:* John, Yoko, and Sean with the extended Ono family in Tokyo.

John found the long visits to Japan to be the healthiest and most tranquil periods of his life. He and Yoko, with Sean perched on his father's bike, cycled about the countryside, freed from the confines of stardom.

Around me he was just a father. I just loved being with him. If we went to stare at a wall I would be happy. . . just his presence was all I needed.

SEAN

NOBODY CONTROLS ME. I'm uncontrollable. The only one that can control me is *me,* and that's just barely possible. And that's the lesson I'm learning. If somebody's going to impress me, whether it be a Maharishi or a Yoko, then there comes a point where the emperor has no clothes 'cause I'm naive, but I'm not stupid. For all you folks out there who think that I'm having the wool pulled over my eyes, well, that's an insult to me. But if you think you know me, or you have some part of me because of the music, and then you think I'm being controlled like a dog on a leash because I do things with her, then screw you, brother or sister, you don't know what's happening. I'm not here for you, I'm here for me and her, and now the baby."

—JOHN

During this time, John rarely played music. When he did, it was most often with his sons, particularly Julian, whose growing talent and shared interest in rock and roll forged a new bond between him and John.

FOR A LONG TIME I wasn't listening to music, to the rock and roll stuff on the radio, because it would cause me to get sweaty—it would bring back memories I didn't want to know about, or I would get that feeling that I'm not alive 'cause I'm not making it. And if it was good, I hated it 'cause I wasn't doing it. And if it was bad, I was furious 'cause I could've done it better. . . .

"My guitar was hung up behind the bed. And I don't think I took it down in five years. . . . Walking away is much harder than carrying on. This must be what guys go through at sixty-five when suddenly they're not supposed to exist anymore, and they are sent out of the office. I hadn't stopped since 1962 until 1973. On demand, on schedule, continuously. It was a case of physician heal thyself. It was more important to face ourselves, and face that reality, than to continue a life of rock and roll show biz. . . .

"The first year I had this sort of feeling in the back of my mind that I ought to [be doing music]. And I'd go through periods of panic, because I was not in *Billboard* or being seen at Studio 54 with Mick and Bianca. I mean, I didn't exist anymore. It would come like a paranoia, and then it would go away, because I'd be involved with the baby. And I realized there was a life without it—a life after death."

—JOHN

215

John, Sean, and Yoko in New York (*above*), Julian in England (*right*) and with Yoko and his father (*overleaf*). Although the press continued to speculate about their lives, John and Yoko maintained a low profile, and John seemed to have quit rock and roll. It was not until a trip to Bermuda in 1980 that John considered returning to the studio.

I WOULD SAY, 'I'm baking bread,' and they'd [friends] say, 'What are you *really* doing?' I'd say, 'I'm looking after the baby.' They'd say, 'But what *else* do you do?' I'd say, 'Are you kidding?!' There were no secret projects in the basement, because bread and babies, as every housewife knows, is a full-time job. . . .

"I don't try and be the God Almighty kind of father figure that is always smiling and such a wonderful father. I'm not into putting out an image of this person who knows all about children. Nobody knows about children. That's the thing. You look in books. There are no real experts. But now I feel as though at least I've put my body where my mouth was and tried to really live up to my own preaching, as it were."

—JOHN

"I THINK JOHN really felt guilty for having been the man who was not aware of what women went through. And so this was like an experience that he really wanted to go through from that point of view."

—YOKO

Starting Over

· · ·

Our life together is so precious together,
We have grown—we have grown.
Although our love is still special,
Let's take a chance and fly away somewhere alone.

STARTING OVER

I HADN'T BEEN in the studio for five years, and Sean was used to me being around all the time. But I started to work, and I got back on a night schedule. So he'd see me at breakfast where I was sort of shredded. And then one day . . . he said, 'You know what I want to be when I grow up?' And I said, 'No, what's that?' He looked me right in the eye and said, 'Just a daddy.' And I said, 'Uh huh, you don't like it that I'm working now, right?' He says, 'Right.' I said, 'Well, I'll tell you something, Sean, it makes me happy to do the music. And I might have more fun with you if I'm happier, right?' He says, 'Uh huh.' And that was the end of that. . . ."

—JOHN

"THE SONG 'BEAUTIFUL BOY' was written for, or about, me. It was also just a story of a father. It was a father—not particularly John, any father—talking to his son, saying, before you cross the street, take my hand. Don't worry because the monster's not there and you can sleep, there's no turtles under the bed going to eat you up. It was just a beautiful song written about all the things that fathers say to their little boys before they go to sleep."

—SEAN

John with Sean (*right*). During his trip to Bermuda John heard a new-wave record in a disco that he thought sounded like some of Yoko's songs. He immediately called Yoko in New York and said, "This time they're ready for us." They went into the studio in August 1980.

I'm trying to go back and enjoy it, as I enjoyed it originally. And it's working.

JOHN

Here and overleaf: John described their new work, *Double Fantasy,* as a "heart play." He and Yoko contributed an equal number of songs—all written over a three-week period—interwoven into a dialogue.

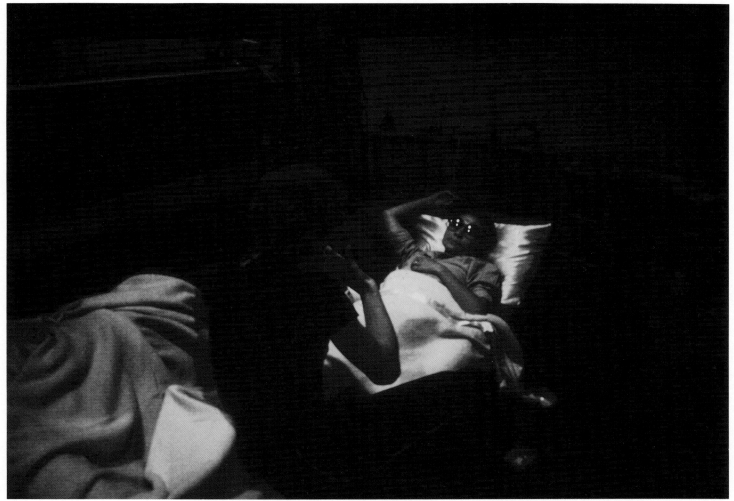

John and Yoko cut twenty-two tracks within a few months in a New York recording studio. *Double Fantasy* was released in November. Though the album's title suggested several meanings, John took it from an exotic orchid he saw in Bermuda.

I F I COULDN'T have worked with her, I wouldn't have bothered. I wouldn't enjoy just putting an album out by myself, having to go to the studio by myself, because, even though I was in a group, I've had that kind of game before. I didn't want to work with another guy. We're presenting ourselves as man and wife and not as sexual objects who sing love songs and are available to the audience. We're presenting ourselves as a couple, and to work with your best friend is a joy."

—JOHN

"WE WERE LIKE TEENAGERS, falling in love again during the making of this album. There was an incredibly strange feeling—'Starting Over' was how he felt, and that's why he wrote the song at the time. We were saying, 'This is crazy, isn't it?' And John was saying, 'We must tell the fans that it gets better after ten years.'"

—YOKO

229

The fall of 1980 was a time of new beginnings. Yoko marked the occasion of *Double Fantasy*'s release by giving John a gold watch inscribed on the back: "To John, Just Like Starting Over. Love Yoko."

He was my husband. He was my lover. He was my friend. He was my partner. And he was an old soldier who fought with me.

YOKO

Maybe we were naive, but still we were very honest about everything we did.

YOKO

With the release of *Double Fantasy*, John and Yoko emerged from their long seclusion. They produced a film of making love as a promotional video in the tradition of *Two Virgins*, in which they showed themselves naked to the world (*following pages*).

W E'RE NOT SELLING ourselves as the perfect couple. We have our problems, we've had our problems, but when I was singing and writing this and working with her, I was visualizing all the people of my age group and singing to them. I hope the young kids like it as well, but I'm really talking to the people that grew up with me. I'm saying, 'Here I am now, how are you, how's your relationship going, did you get through it all, weren't the seventies a drag, here we are, well, let's try and make the eighties good, you know.' It's not out of our control, I still believe in love. I still believe in peace. . . . Where there's life, there's hope."

—JOHN

Now John and Yoko began to reappear in New York, dining out, greeting fans, strolling down the streets. John enjoyed the relative anonymity he had even as a celebrity. "I went through that period where I actually couldn't go anywhere, and so now, it's heaven." *Above:* John and Yoko in Central Park and (*right*) walking alongside the Dakota. They talked openly to the press about their past, their renewed inspiration, and their future plans, which included a world tour.

My role in society, or any artist or poet's role, is to try and express what we all feel. Not to tell people how to feel. Not as a preacher, not as a leader, but as a reflection of us all.

JOHN

On the night of December 8, 1980, John Lennon, returning home with Yoko from a recording session, was shot in front of his New York apartment building. The police rushed him to Roosevelt Hospital, where he was pronounced dead on arrival. As news of his death spread throughout the city, crowds of bereaved fans began gathering around the Dakota to pay homage to the man whose music and life had touched so many. Yoko sent the mourners a simple message: "John loved and prayed for the human race. Please do the same for him."

Imagine there's no Heaven
It's easy if you try
No Hell below us
Above us only sky
Imagine all the people
Living for today
Imagine there's no countries
It isn't hard to do
Nothing to kill or die for
And no religion too
Imagine all the people
Living life in peace
You may say I'm a dreamer
But I'm not the only one
I hope someday you'll join us
And the world will live as one
Imagine no possessions
I wonder if you can
No need for greed or hunger
A brotherhood of man
Imagine all the people
Sharing all the world
You may say I'm a dreamer
But I'm not the only one
I hope someday you'll join us
And the world will live as one

IMAGINE

Chronology

...

October 9, 1940   John Lennon is born during a bombing raid at Oxford Street Maternity Hospital, Liverpool, to Julia Stanley and Alfred Lennon.

1945   Julia, separated from Alfred, entrusts John to the care of her sister Mary Elizabeth Stanley Smith, "Aunt Mimi," who with her husband George raise John in a house on Menlove Avenue. John attends Dovedale Primary School.

June 5, 1952   George Smith dies suddenly of a brain hemorrhage.

Fall 1952   John enters Quarry Bank High School.

1956   Aunt Mimi buys John a guitar at Frank Hessy's music store. His incessant playing prompts her to say, "The guitar's all very well as a hobby, John, but you'll never make a living out of it." John forms his first group, the Quarrymen, with pals Pete Shotton, Nigel Whalley, and Ivan Vaughan.

July 6, 1957   John meets Paul McCartney at the Woolton Parish Church in Liverpool during a performance by the Quarrymen. John, impressed by Paul's ability to tune a guitar and by his knowledge of song lyrics, asks Paul if he wants to join the group as a lead guitarist.

September 1957   John enrolls at the Liverpool College of Art, where he meets Cynthia Powell.

February 1958   Paul introduces George Harrison to the Quarrymen at a basement teen club called the Morgue. George joins the group.

July 15, 1958   Julia Lennon is killed, run over by an off-duty policeman.

1958   John writes his first song, "Hello Little Girl." It will be recorded by the Beatles at their 1962 audition for Decca Records.

July 1960   John drops out of art college to work full-time with his band.

August 1960   The Beatles debut in Hamburg, West Germany, with Stu Sutcliffe on bass and drummer Pete Best. They hone their craft in the tawdry, sometimes violent Reeperbahn, Hamburg's renowned nightclub district. While in Hamburg, they are introduced to Preludin, a stimulant that keeps them going through marathon performances for boisterous German crowds. When the Beatles return to England, Sutcliffe remains in Germany.

January 1961   The Beatles debut at the Cavern Club.

Summer/Fall 1961   John writes the first brief biography of the Beatles for *Mersey Beat,* a local music newspaper. It is followed by a series of weekly columns containing Lennon stories, poems, and cartoons.

November–December 1961   Local record store manager Brian Epstein is introduced to the Beatles at the Cavern. A month later Epstein signs a contract to manage them.

Spring 1962   Epstein transforms the Beatles' appearance. He trades in their black leather outfits for shiny gray lounge suits with velvet collars, cloth-covered buttons, and thin lapels.

April 10, 1962   Stu Sutcliffe dies of a brain hemorrhage the same week the Beatles are scheduled to return to the Star Club in Hamburg.

June 1962   The Beatles audition for George Martin, a record producer at Parlophone/EMI. Martin wants to replace drummer Pete Best. Within two months Best is out and Richard "Ringo" Starkey joins the group.

August 23, 1962   Cynthia Powell, pregnant, marries John at Mt. Pleasant Register Office in Liverpool.

September 4–11, 1962   The Beatles record their first songs at EMI Studios, St. Johns Wood, London. George Martin is the producer.

December 1962–March 1963   "Love Me Do"—the first Beatles hit—peaks on the British charts at number 17. It is soon followed by "Please Please Me," the group's first number one single. A week later the album *Please Please Me* is released and soon becomes their first number one LP.

April 8, 1963   John Charles Julian Lennon is born to Cynthia and John at Sefton General Hospital, Liverpool. The birth, like the marriage, is kept secret from Beatle fans at Brian's urging.

August 3, 1963   The Beatles play their farewell show at the Cavern Club, having logged almost three hundred performances there.

November 4, 1963   The Beatles appear at the Royal Variety Performance before the Queen Mother, Princess Margaret, and Lord Snowden.

November 1963/January 1964   Beatlemania is now officially underway in Britain, as announced in the London *Daily Mirror.*

February 7, 1964 The Beatles begin their first U.S. tour.

February 9 and 16, 1964 The Beatles headline twice on the "Ed Sullivan Show" on CBS, for $3,500 a performance.

March 1964 Shooting begins on the Beatles' first feature film, *A Hard Day's Night,* as "Can't Buy Me Love" tops the charts both in Britain and America.

March 23, 1964 John's first book, *In His Own Write,* is published and becomes an instant best-seller.

July 6, 1964 The world premiere of *A Hard Day's Night* takes place in London. Critics and audiences generally acclaim the film, directed by Richard Lester.

August 18–September 15, 1964 The Beatles tour America.

August 28, 1964 Bob Dylan turns on the foursome to marijuana at the Delmonico Hotel in New York City.

January 1965 John composes "Help!", the title song for the Beatles' second film. He later confides the lyrics are a plaintive cry for help and a clue to the confusion and despondency he feels.

Spring 1965 John, Cynthia, George Harrison, and Patti Boyd inadvertently take their first LSD trip when a dentist-friend of Harrison's spikes their coffee.

June 24, 1965 John's second book, *A Spaniard in the Works,* is published.

July 29, 1965 *Help!* has its world premiere in London's West End. Reviews hail the Beatles as "modern Marx Brothers."

August 1965 The Beatles meet Elvis Presley at his home in Bel Air. Not knowing their individual names, Elvis refers to each as "Beatle."

August 15, 1965 The Beatles play in front of almost 60,000 fans at Shea Stadium in New York, the largest audience in history. The take is $304,000, the largest one-night gross for a concert event to date.

October 26, 1965 The Beatles are awarded Britain's prestigious MBE (Members of the Order of the British Empire), a particularly unique honor for rock artists. John comments, "I thought you had to drive tanks and win wars to get the MBE."

July 1966 John's comments on the state of Christianity, published in an interview in London's *Evening Standard* in March, spark a firestorm of protest in the U.S. on the eve of the Beatles' 1966 American tour.

Summer 1966 Problems plague the Beatles' world tour. Right-wing militants threaten them in Tokyo. In the Philippines there are violent street demonstrations after the group allegedly snubs the president's wife.

August 8, 1966 The *Revolver* album is released.

August 29, 1966 After their concert at San Francisco's Candlestick Park, the Beatles declare this to be their final world tour.

September/October 1966 John makes his first appearance away from the Beatles in the role of Private Gripweed, a WWI soldier in Richard Lester's film *How I Won the War.* John writes "Strawberry Fields Forever" while filming.

November 1966 Yoko Ono and John Lennon meet for the first time at a preview of her art show Exhibition #2 at Indica Gallery in London.

June 1, 1967 *Sgt. Pepper's Lonely Hearts Club Band* is released.

August 27, 1967 Brian Epstein dies of an apparent overdose of drugs while the Beatles are in a seminar on transcendental meditation with the Maharishi Mahesh Yogi in Bangor, North Wales.

September 1967 John writes "I Am the Walrus" while under the influence of LSD. The Beatles' film *Magical Mystery Tour* airs on the BBC in December and is received with a resounding blast from the critics. John anonymously sponsors Yoko's Half a Wind Show (subtitled Yoko Plus Me) at London's Lisson Gallery.

December 7, 1967 The Beatles open the Apple Boutique at 94 Baker Street, London.

Spring 1968 The Beatles attend a three-month course on transcendental meditation with the Maharishi in Rishikesh, India. While there, John writes "Yer Blues," "I'm So Tired," "Revolution," "Dear Prudence," and "Sexy Sadie." Yoko and he begin to exchange letters.

May 1968 Apple Corp., Ltd., officially begins operating in London. It is an attempt on the group's part to take the reins of their own creative and economic destiny and, in John's words, "to wrest control from the men in suits." Later that month John invites Yoko to his house in Weybridge. They make experimental tapes all night and make love at dawn.

May 1968–June 15, 1968 John and Yoko exhibit their first official joint venture at the Arts Lab, Drury Lane, London. Soon after, they plant acorns outside Coventry Cathedral as a conceptual "living art sculpture."

July 1, 1968 John holds his first art exhibition, entitled You Are Here—To Yoko from John, with Love. The show includes a circular white canvas and assorted charities' collection boxes. Before the show 360 white balloons are released simultaneously into the sky.

Summer 1968 John moves out of his house in Weybridge and moves into Ringo Starr's apartment in Montague Square with Yoko.

July 31, 1968 The Apple Boutique closes after a liquidation sale in which the remaining inventory is given away.

October 18, 1968 John and Yoko are arrested and charged with possession of cannabis. They are remanded to Marylebone Magistrates' Court, and released on bail.

November 8, 1968 A divorce is granted to John and Cynthia Lennon. Cynthia is reportedly given a £100,000 settlement.

November 1968 John pleads guilty to marijuana possession charges. He pays a nominal fine but continues to insist that the drugs were planted by a "head-hunting" cop. Yoko suffers a miscarriage and is hospitalized at Queen Charlotte's Hospital, London. John sleeps on the floor next to her bed. Just before the baby dies, John records its heartbeat. Later he christens the baby John Ono Lennon II.

November 11, 1968 John and Yoko release their first album together: *Unfinished Music No. 1: Two Virgins.* The cover, a full frontal shot of them naked, is banned. EMI refuses to release the album which is later distributed by a small independent label.

November 1968 Within one month, John and Yoko produce three avant-garde films: *Two Virgins,* a nineteen-minute short superimposing their faces; *Number Five,* aka *Smile,* originally a three-minute film of John's smiling face that is slowed down to fifty-two minutes; and *Rape,* Yoko's portrait of a woman pursued by a relentless camera.

December 1968 John makes a guest appearance on "Rock and Roll Circus," an ill-fated Rolling Stones TV special, and performs "Yer Blues." He is backed by Keith Richards, Eric Clapton, and Mitch Mitchell.

January 30, 1969 The Beatles' last performance as a group is on the roof of the Apple building, during the filming of *Let It Be*. John thinks Paul intends his lyrics, "get back to where you once belonged," for Yoko, who is at John's side during the session.

February 2, 1969 Yoko Ono is divorced from Tony Cox.

February 3, 1969 The Beatles argue about appointing American businessman Allen Klein as their business advisor. John, impressed that Klein can quote from his songs, feels Klein has an instinctive grasp of the group's problems. Paul disagrees and prefers the Beatles' business to be handled by his future wife's father Lee Eastman, a prominent New York lawyer.

March 2, 1969 John and Yoko hold their first public performance together at an avant-garde jazz concert at Lady Mitchell Hall, Cambridge, England. Excerpts from the recording are later included on the album *Unfinished Music No. 2*.

March 20, 1969 John and Yoko marry in Gibraltar.

March 25–31, 1969 They celebrate their honeymoon by hosting their first "bed-in" at the Amsterdam Hilton. The seven-day event is designed as a "commercial for peace."

April 22, 1969 John officially changes his name from John Winston Lennon to John Ono Lennon.

May 9, 1969 John and Yoko release *Unfinished Music No. 2: Life with the Lions* on Apple's newly-formed avant-garde label Zapple.

May 26–June 2, 1969 John and Yoko conduct a bed-in at the Queen Elizabeth Hotel in Montreal. They hold over sixty interviews with the press. The couple records "Give Peace a Chance" with Tommy Smothers, Timothy Leary, and the Canadian chapter of the Hare Krishnas. The event is marked by an acrimonious debate with conservative American cartoonist Al Capp.

June 4, 1969 "The Ballad of John and Yoko," the couple's autobiographical account of their marriage and life together, is released and credited to Lennon – McCartney. Though John wrote the song, the drumming, later overdubbed, is Paul's.

July–August 1969 The Beatles record *Abbey Road*.

August 1969 John and Yoko move to Tittenhurst Park, a four-hundred-acre estate in Ascot.

Fall 1969 The Beatles lose control of all their songs when the majority owner of their music publishing business, Northern Songs, sells 50 percent of the company to ATV.

September 1969 "Two Evenings with John and Yoko" is presented at the New Cinema Club, London. The film festival includes the world premiere of *Self Portrait*, a forty-two-minute film documenting John's penis rising from a flaccid to erect state in slow motion.

September 12, 1969 John appears live at the Toronto Rock 'n' Roll Revival concert, flanked by Eric Clapton, Klaus Voormann, and Alan White. Yoko appears sitting onstage in a canvas bag. *The Plastic Ono Band—Live Peace in Toronto*, is released in December.

September 1969 John makes a promotional film for "Cold Turkey," his newest single. Two months later he returns his MBE award to Buckingham Palace, in protest against British involvement in Biafra, the government's support for the U.S. in Vietnam, and "Cold Turkey"'s poor performance on the charts.

October 9, 1969 Yoko suffers a second miscarriage at the Kings College Hospital in Denmark Hill, London, on John's twenty-ninth birthday.

October 20, 1969 *The Wedding Album*, third in a series of John and Yoko's autobiographical albums, is released. The album contains pictures of the couple's Gibraltar wedding and Amsterdam bed-in.

December 16 "War Is Over! If You Want It" billboards go up in eleven cities around the world as a Christmas message from John and Yoko.

December 16–20, 1969 John and Yoko spend five days at Ronnie Hawkins's farm near Toronto. They set up camp on behalf of John's peace campaign for the intended Mosport Park, Canada, Peace Festival.

December 22, 1969 John and Yoko meet with Prime Minister Pierre Trudeau as Lennon promotes his Acorns for Peace project.

December 29, 1969 John and Yoko fly to Aalborg, Denmark, to visit Yoko's daughter, Kyoko, who is living with Tony Cox and his wife Melinda.

January–February 1970 Eight of John's Bag One lithographs, some of them showing him locked in intimate sexual embraces with Yoko, are seized from the London Arts Gallery by police for obscenity.

February 1970 Yoko's book *Grapefruit* is published in the U.S.

February 4, 1970 John and Yoko donate their shorn hair to Michael X, a Black Power revolutionary in Britain, to be auctioned at a fund-raiser for Black House, a center for black culture in North London.

April 10, 1970 Undercutting John, who has promised not to announce his intended departure from the Beatles, Paul announces at a press conference that he has left the group due to "personal, business, and musical differences." His first solo album, *McCartney*, is subsequently released with considerable fanfare.

August 1, 1970 Yoko suffers her third miscarriage.

December 1970 While visiting New York City, John and Yoko meet with Jonas Mekas, underground filmmaker, and shoot the films *Up Your Legs Forever* and *Fly*.

December 30, 1970 Paul begins High Court proceedings to end the Beatles' partnership. A court trial begins the following month.

June 6, 1971 John and Yoko appear in concert with Frank Zappa and the Mothers of Invention at the Fillmore East in New York.

July 1971 John records *Imagine* in his studio at Tittenhurst Park. The title track is inspired by a message in Yoko's book *Grapefruit*.

Mid-1971 John and Yoko hire a team of private detectives to find Kyoko, who is kept out of sight by Yoko's former husband Tony Cox. The Lennons finally find the little girl at a children's camp in Majorca, Spain. As they take the child back to their hotel, John and Yoko are arrested by police on kidnapping charges.

August 1971 The Lennons obtain a legal writ of custody in order to retrieve Kyoko. They soon rent an apartment in Greenwich Village, New York.

October 9–27, 1971 Yoko's exhibition This Is Not Here is held at Everson Museum of Art, Syracuse. John is a guest artist.

October 1971 John and Yoko participate in a demonstration on behalf of the Onondaga Indians in Syracuse.

November 1971 John performs a benefit concert at the Apollo Theatre for the families of inmates at Attica State Prison.

December 1971 John and Yoko appear at the University of Michigan for a benefit for John Sinclair, founder of the White Panthers, who is serving a ten-year prison sentence for marijuana possession. Later that month John and Yoko film *Clock,* a one-hour feature that focuses on a French clock in the lobby of the St. Regis Hotel in New York. They produce two 60-second shorts entitled *Freedom Films.* John's *Ten for Two*, his film of the Ann Arbor benefit concert for John Sinclair, is not shown in the U.S., due to Lennon's ongoing immigration problems.

December 22, 1971 A judge awards custody of Kyoko, now renamed Rosemary, to her father, who has become a born-again Christian. Yoko is permitted to see her child frequently, but she must post a $20,000 bond—in case she "kidnaps" the girl again. Her ex-husband refuses to let John and Yoko take the child to their apartment over the Christmas holidays. Later Cox vanishes, along with his wife and Kyoko. They are never seen again by the Lennons.

January 1972 The staff of the U.S. Senate Internal Security Subcommittee of the Judiciary Committee prepares and submits to Senator Strom Thurmond a memo about John's involvement with the radicals Jerry Rubin, Abbie Hoffman, and Rennie Davis.

February 4, 1972 Senator Strom Thurmond suggests in a secret memo to Attorney General John Mitchell that John be deported.

February 29–March 6, 1972 John's U.S. non-immigrant visa expires. An extension is granted on March 1 and is revoked five days later. Hearings on deportation proceedings are held in subsequent weeks.

June 12, 1972 *Some Time in New York City* is released.

August 30, 1972 John and Yoko give a special performance for the One to One Organization (which collects funds to house retarded children). At the Madison Square Garden concert in New York (aired on ABC-TV on December 15), they receive a five-minute standing ovation. The charity receives $1.5 million from the event. Also, John and Yoko's film short *Erection* has its world premiere. The nineteen-minute film depicts the construction of the International Hotel, using hundreds of photos taken over an eighteen-month period.

December 23, 1972 John and Yoko's *Imagine,* their eighty-one-minute color film with soundtrack from the *Imagine* album, appears on U.S. television. Guest artists include George Harrison, Fred Astaire, Phil Spector, Dick Cavett, and Andy Warhol.

March 2, 1973 Judge Ira Fieldsteel rules that John must leave the U.S. voluntarily within the next sixty days or face deportation. Yoko is granted permanent residency. One month later an appeal is filed.

April 1973 John and Yoko purchase an apartment at the Dakota on Central Park West and 72nd Street in New York.

Fall 1973 For the first time since they met in 1968, John and Yoko agree to separate. John travels to Los Angeles. He called his eighteen-month separation from Yoko his "lost weekend."

October 1973 John sues the Immigration and Naturalization Service under the Freedom of Information Act, seeking evidence of prejudice and wiretapping. During this

time, he persuades Phil Spector to produce his rock and roll oldies album.

November 1973 John, Paul, and George sue Allen Klein. "The only thing that has prevented us from getting together again," declares Paul, "has been Klein's contractual hold over the Beatles' name. When he's out of the way, there is no real reason why we shouldn't get together again." John's album *Mind Games* is released.

March 1974 While producing Harry Nilsson's *Pussy Cats* album in Los Angeles, John makes headlines during a Smothers Brothers performance at the Troubadour. Drunk on brandy alexanders, he heckles Dick Smothers and is physically removed from the club.

July 17, 1974 The INS Board denies John's appeal and orders him to leave the country within sixty days. He again appeals.

August 1974 John records the *Walls and Bridges* album, writing ten of the songs in a single week.

October 21–25, 1974 John returns to Los Angeles to record more songs for his *Rock 'n' Roll* album. This time he produces the songs himself.

November 28, 1974 Lennon agrees to accompany Elton John on stage at Madison Square Garden. It is John's last concert appearance. Lennon is unaware that Yoko is in the audience and later they meet backstage.

January 1975 John and Yoko are reunited. The Beatles' final dissolution takes place in London.

February 1975 Yoko becomes pregnant.

October 9, 1975 Sean Taro Ono Lennon is born at New York Hospital on John's thirty-fifth birthday. John is ecstatic. He exclaims, "I feel higher than the Empire State Building."

October 24, 1975 *Shaved Fish,* a collection of John's songs from 1969–1975, is released.

July 27, 1976 John's application to remain in the U.S. as a permanent resident is approved at a special hearing.

1977–1979 The Lennons extend their real estate holdings by buying five co-ops in the Dakota, four dairy farms in upstate New York, a house in Palm Beach, Florida, and a mountain retreat in New York State. During this time Yoko, John, and Sean visit Japan for extended family vacations. John and Yoko take out full-page ads in many leading newspapers, including *The New York Times* and the *Los Angeles Times.* The message: "Give us a little more time to figure out what we're going to do." The majority of John's time is spent as a "househusband"—taking care of Sean and baking bread—while Yoko handles their business affairs. She negotiates a reported $5 million settlement with Allen Klein.

June 1980 John takes a sailing trip to Bermuda. It is his first time at sea in a small boat. He sails three thousand miles in seven days. In Bermuda with Sean, John begins writing songs again.

October 23, 1980 John's first new single, "(Just Like) Starting Over," is released.

November 17, 1980 The *Double Fantasy* album is released internationally. Plans are discussed for a world tour.

December 8, 1980 John and Yoko return to the Dakota in their limousine, after a recording session. As John walks toward the entryway of the building, a deranged assailant, Mark David Chapman, fires five shots, hitting John in the chest. By the time Yoko and police rush him to Roosevelt Hospital's emergency room, John Lennon is dead.

Discography

. . .

The following is based on Capitol Records' release dates and issues of Beatles recordings in the United States and on all subsequent U.S. releases of Lennon recordings, including as a Beatle on Apple Records and as a solo artist recording for Capitol/EMI, Polydor, and Geffen records. This discography includes both single releases and album packages, but does not include reissues.

BEATLES ALBUMS

Meet the Beatles! (Capitol, 1/20/64): I Want to Hold Your Hand; I Saw Her Standing There; This Boy; It Won't Be Long; All I've Got to Do; All My Loving; Don't Bother Me; Little Child; Till There Was You; Hold Me Tight; I Wanna Be Your Man; Not a Second Time.

The Beatles' Second Album (Capitol, 4/10/64): Long Tall Sally; I Call Your Name; Please Mr. Postman; I'll Get You; She Loves You; Roll Over, Beethoven; Thank You Girl; You Really Got a Hold on Me; Devil in Her Heart; Money (That's What I Want); You Can't Do That.

A Hard Day's Night (Capitol, 6/26/64): A Hard Day's Night; Tell Me Why; I'll Cry Instead; I'm Happy Just to Dance with You; I Should Have Known Better; If I Fell; And I Love Her; Ringo's Theme (This Boy); Can't Buy Me Love.

Something New (Capitol 7/20/64): I'll Cry Instead; Things We Said Today; Anytime at All; When I Get Home; Slow Down; Matchbox; Tell Me Why; And I Love Her; I'm Happy Just to Dance with You; If I Fell; Komm, Gib Mir Deine Hand.

Beatles '65 (Capitol 12/15/64): No Reply; I'm a Loser; Baby's in Black; Rock and Roll Music; I'll Follow the Sun; Mr. Moonlight; Honey Don't; I'll Be Back; She's a Woman; I Feel Fine; Everybody's Trying to Be My Baby.

The Early Beatles (Capitol, 3/22/65): Love Me Do; Twist and Shout; Anna (Go to Him); Chains; Boys; Ask Me Why; Please Please Me; P.S. I Love You; Baby, It's You; A Taste of Honey; Do You Want to Know a Secret.

Beatles VI (Capitol 6/14/65): Eight Days a Week; Kansas City/Hey Hey Hey; You Like Me Too Much; Bad Boy; I Don't Want to Spoil the Party; Words of Love; What You're Doing; Yes It Is; Dizzy Miss Lizzie; Tell Me What You See; Every Little Thing.

Help! (Capitol, 8/13/65): Help!; The Night Before; You've Got to Hide Your Love Away; I Need You; Another Girl; Ticket to Ride; You're Gonna Lose That Girl.

Rubber Soul (Capitol, 12/6/65): I've Just Seen a Face; Norwegian Wood (This Bird Has Flown); You Won't See Me; Think for Yourself; The Word; Michelle; It's Only Love; Girl; I'm Looking Through You; In My Life; Wait; Run for Your Life.

"Yesterday" . . . and Today (Capitol, 6/20/66): Drive My Car; I'm Only Sleeping; Nowhere Man; Dr. Robert; Yesterday; Act Naturally; And Your Bird Can Sing; If I Needed Someone; We Can Work It Out; What Goes On?; Day Tripper.

Revolver (Capitol, 8/8/66): Taxman; Eleanor Rigby; Love You To; Here, There and Everywhere; Yellow Submarine; She Said, She Said; Good Day Sunshine; For No One; I Want to Tell You; Got to Get You into My Life; Tomorrow Never Knows.

Sgt. Pepper's Lonely Hearts Club Band (Capitol, 6/2/67): Sgt. Pepper's Lonely Hearts Club Band; With a Little Help from My Friends; Lucy in the Sky with Diamonds; Getting Better; Fixing a Hole; She's Leaving Home; Being for the Benefit of Mr. Kite!; Within You, Without You; When I'm Sixty-four; Lovely Rita; Good Morning, Good Morning;   A Day in the Life.

Magical Mystery Tour (Capitol, 11/27/67): Magical Mystery Tour; The Fool on the Hill; Flying; Blue Jay Way; Your Mother Should Know; I Am the Walrus; Hello Goodbye; Strawberry Fields Forever; Penny Lane; Baby You're a Rich Man; All You Need Is Love.

The Beatles ("The White Album") (Apple 11/25/68): Back in the U.S.S.R.; Dear Prudence; Glass Onion; Ob-La-Di, Ob-La-Da; Wild Honey Pie; The Continuing Story of Bungalow Bill; While My Guitar Gently Weeps; Happiness Is a Warm Gun; Martha My Dear; I'm So Tired; Blackbird; Piggies; Rocky Raccoon; Don't Pass Me By; Why Don't We Do It in the Road?; I Will; Julia; Birthday; Yer Blues; Mother Nature's Son; Everybody's Got Something to Hide, Except Me and My Monkey; Sexy Sadie; Helter Skelter; Long, Long, Long; Revolution 1; Honey Pie; Savoy Truffle; Cry Baby Cry; Revolution 9; Goodnight.

Yellow Submarine (Apple, 1/13/69): Yellow Submarine; Only a Northern Song; All Together Now; Hey Bulldog; It's All Too Much; All You Need Is Love.

Abbey Road (Apple, 10/1/69): Come Together; Something; Maxwell's Silver Hammer; Oh! Darling; Octopus's Garden; I Want You (She's So Heavy); Here Comes the Sun; Because; You Never Give Me Your Money; Sun King; Mean Mr. Mustard; Polythene Pam; She Came in through the Bathroom Window; Golden Slumbers; Carry That Weight; The End; Her Majesty.

Hey Jude (Apple, 2/26/70): Can't Buy Me Love; I Should Have Known Better; Paperback Writer; Rain; Lady Madonna; Revolution; Hey Jude; Old Brown Shoe; Don't Let Me Down; The Ballad of John and Yoko.

Let It Be (Apple 5/18/70): Two of Us; Dig a Pony; Across the Universe; I Me Mine; Let It Be; Maggie Mae; I've Got a Feeling; One after 909; The Long and Winding Road; For You Blue; Get Back.

BEATLES SINGLES

Please Please Me/Ask Me Why (Vee Jay, 2/25/63)

From Me To You/Thank You Girl (Vee Jay, 5/27/63)

She Loves You/I'll Get You (Swan, 9/16/63)

I Want to Hold Your Hand/I Saw Her Standing There (Capitol, 1/13/64)

Please Please Me/From Me to You (Vee Jay, 1/30/64)

Twist and Shout/There's a Place (Tollie, 3/2/64)

Can't Buy Me Love/You Can't Do That (Capitol, 3/16/64)

Do You Want to Know a Secret/Thank You Girl (Vee Jay, 3/23/64)

Love Me Do/P.S. I Love You (Tollie, 4/27/64)

Sie Liebt Dich/I'll Get You (Swan, 5/21/64)

A Hard Day's Night/I Should Have Known Better (Capitol, 7/13/64)

I'll Cry Instead/I'm Happy Just to Dance with You (Capitol, 7/20/64)

And I Love Her/If I Fell (Capitol, 7/20/64)

Do You Want to Know a Secret/Thank You Girl (Oldies, 8/10/64)

Please Please Me/From Me to You (Oldies, 8/10/64)

Love Me Do/P.S. I Love You (Oldies, 8/10/64)

Twist and Shout/There's a Place (Oldies, 8/10/64)

Slow Down/Matchbox (Capitol, 8/24/64)

I Feel Fine/She's a Woman (Capitol, 11/23/64)

Eight Days a Week/I Don't Want to Spoil the Party (Capitol, 2/15/65)

Ticket to Ride/Yes It Is (Capitol, 4/14/65)

Help!/I'm Down (Capitol, 7/19/65)

Yesterday/Act Naturally (Capitol, 9/13/65)

We Can Work It Out/Day Tripper (Capitol, 12/6/65)

Nowhere Man/What Goes On (Capitol, 2/21/66)

Paperback Writer/Rain (Capitol, 5/30/66)

Yellow Submarine/Eleanor Rigby (Capitol, 8/8/66)

Penny Lane/Strawberry Fields Forever (Capitol, 2/13/67)

All You Need Is Love/Baby You're a Rich Man (Capitol, 7/17/67)

Hello Goodbye/I Am the Walrus (Capitol, 11/27/67)

Lady Madonna/The Inner Light (Capitol, 3/18/68)

Hey Jude/Revolution (Apple, 8/26/68)

Get Back/Don't Let Me Down (Apple, 5/5/69)

The Ballad of John and Yoko/Old Brown Shoe (Apple, 6/4/69)

Give Peace a Chance/Remember Love (Apple, 7/7/69)

Something/Come Together (Apple, 10/6/69)

Cold Turkey/Don't Worry Kyoko (Apple, 10/20/69)

Let It Be/You Know My Name (Look Up the Number) (Apple, 3/11/70)

The Long And Winding Road/For You Blue (Apple, 5/11/70)

JOHN LENNON SOLO ALBUMS

Unfinished Music No. 1—Two Virgins[1] (Apple, 11/11/68): Two Virgins No. 1; Together; Two Virgins No. 2; Two Virgins No. 3; Two Virgins No. 4; Two Virgins No. 5; Two Virgins No. 6; Hushabye Hushabye; Two Virgins No. 7; Two Virgins No. 8; Two Virgins No. 9; Two Virgins No. 10.

Unfinished Music No. 2—Life with the Lions[1] (Zapple 5/26/69): Cambridge 1969; No Bed for Beatle John; Baby's Heartbeat; Two Minutes Silence; Radio Play.

The Wedding Album[1] (Apple, 10/20/69): John and Yoko; Amsterdam.

The Plastic Ono Band—Live Peace in Toronto (Apple, 12/12/69): Blue Suede Shoes; Money (That's What I Want); Dizzy Miss Lizzie; Yer Blues; Cold Turkey; Give Peace a Chance; Don't Worry Kyoko (Mummy's Only Looking for a Hand in the Snow); John, John (Let's Hope for Peace).

John Lennon/Plastic Ono Band (Apple, 12/11/70): Mother; Hold On John; I Found Out; Working Class Hero; Isolation; Remember; Love; Well Well Well; Look at Me; God; My Mummy's Dead.

Imagine (Apple, 9/9/71): Imagine; Crippled Inside; Jealous Guy; It's So Hard; I Don't Want to Be a Soldier, Mama I Don't Wanna Die; Give Me Some Truth; Oh My Love; How Do You Sleep?; How?; Oh Yoko!.

Some Time in New York City (Apple, 6/12/72): Woman Is the Nigger of the World; Sisters, O Sisters; Attica State; Born in a Prison; New York City; Sunday Bloody Sunday; The Luck of the Irish; John Sinclair; Angela; We're All Water; Cold Turkey; Don't Worry Kyoko; Well (Baby Please Don't Go); Jamrag; Scumbag; Aü.

Mind Games (Apple, 10/29/73; rereleased by Capitol 10/80): Mind Games; Tight As; Aisumasen (I'm Sorry); One Day (At a Time); Bring On the Lucie (Freeda Peeple); Nutopian International Anthem; Intuition; Out the Blue; Only People; I Know (I Know); You Are Here; Meat City.

Walls and Bridges (Apple, 9/26/74): Going Down on Love; Whatever Gets You thru the Night; Old Dirt Road; What You Got; Bless You; Scared; No.9 Dream; Surprise Surprise (Sweet Bird of Paradox); Steel and Glass; Beef Jerky; Nobody Loves You (When You're Down and Out); Ya Ya.

Rock 'n' Roll[2] (Apple, 2/17/75); rereleased by Capitol, 10/80): Be-Bop-a-Lula; Stand by Me; Medley: Ready Teddy/Rip It Up; You Can't Catch Me; Ain't That a Shame; Do You Want to Dance; Sweet Little Sixteen; Slippin' and Slidin'; Peggy Sue; Medley: Bring It On Home to Me/Send Me Some Lovin'; Bony Moronie; Ya Ya; Just Because.

Shaved Fish (Apple, 10/24/75): Give Peace a Chance; Cold Turkey; Instant Karma!; Power to the People; Mother; Woman Is the Nigger of the World; Imagine; Whatever Gets You thru the Night; Mind Games; No. 9 Dream; Happy Xmas (War Is Over); Reprise: Give Peace a Chance.

Double Fantasy (Geffen, 11/17/80): (Just Like) Starting Over; Kiss Kiss Kiss; Cleanup Time; Give Me Something; I'm Losing You; I'm Moving On; Beautiful Boy (Darling Boy); Watching the Wheels; I'm Your Angel; Woman; Beautiful Boys; Dear Yoko; Every Man Has a Woman Who Loves Him; Hard Times Are Over.

Milk and Honey (Polydor, 1/84): I'm Stepping Out; Sleepless Night; I Don't Want to Face It; Don't Be Scared; Nobody Told Me; O' Sanity; Borrowed Time; Your Hands; (Forgive Me) My Little Flower Princess; Let Me Count the Ways; Grow Old with Me; You're the One.

John Lennon—Live in New York City (Capitol, 1986): New York City; It's So Hard; Woman Is the Nigger of the World; Well, Well, Well; Instant Karma!; Mother; Come Together; Imagine; Cold Turkey; Hound Dog; Give Peace a Chance.

John Lennon—Menlove Avenue (Capitol, 1986): Here We Go Again; Rock 'n' Roll People; Angel Baby; Since My Baby Left Me; To Know Her Is to Love Her; Steel and Glass; Scared; Old Dirt Road; Nobody Loves You When You're Down and Out; Bless You.

JOHN LENNON SOLO SINGLES

Instant Karma!/Who Has Seen the Wind? (Apple, 2/20/70)

Mother/Why (Apple, 12/28/70)

Power to the People/Touch Me (Apple, 3/22/71)

Imagine/It's So Hard (Apple, 10/11/71)

Happy Xmas (War Is Over)/Listen, the Snow Is Falling (Apple, 12/1/71)

Woman Is the Nigger of the World/Sisters, O Sisters (Apple, 4/24/72)

Mind Games/Meat City (Apple, 10/29/73)

Whatever Gets You thru the Night/Beef Jerky (Apple, 9/23/74)

No. 9 Dream/What You Got (Apple, 12/16/74)

Stand by Me/Move Over Ms. L (Apple, 3/10/75)

(Just Like) Starting Over/Kiss Kiss Kiss (Geffen, 10/23/80)

Woman/Beautiful Boys (Geffen, 1/12/81)

Watching the Wheels/I'm Your Angel (Geffen, 3/13/81)

(Just Like) Starting Over/Woman (Geffen, 6/5/81)

Watching the Wheels/Beautiful Boy (Darling Boy) (Geffen, 11/4/81)

Happy Xmas (War Is Over)/Beautiful Boy (Darling Boy) (Geffen, 11/17/82)

Nobody Told Me/O' Sanity (Polydor, 1/84)

Borrowed Time/Your Hands (Polydor, 3/84)

I'm Stepping Out/Sleepless Night (Polydor, 7/84)

Every Man Has a Woman Who Loves Him/It's Alright[3] (Polydor, 11/84)

[1]All songs by John and Yoko. [2]All songs written by other artists. [3]Written by Yoko Ono.

Credits

. . .

QUOTE CREDITS

The quotes used throughout the book were taken from the following sources:

Andrew Solt interview with Mary Elizabeth Smith (Aunt Mimi), June 3, 1987, pages 17, 18, 20, 23, 25, 32, 55. Andrew Solt interview with Cynthia Lennon, January 19, 1988, pages 28, 32, 65, 79, 82, 97, 112. Andrew Solt interview with Elliot Mintz, January 21, 1988, pages 95, 184, 188. Andrew Solt interview with Julian Lennon, January 20, 1988, pages 108, 200. Andrew Solt interview with Yoko Ono Lennon, January 21, 1988, pages 120, 123, 125, 166, 171, 172, 181 (first paragraph), 216, 229, 231. Andrew Solt interview with Sean Lennon, January 21, 1988, pages 196, 200, 206, 210, 222. All interviews courtesy of Andrew Solt Productions.

Playboy interview with John Lennon and Yoko Ono, conducted by David Sheff, September 1980. Copyright © 1981 by *Playboy*. Used by permission. All rights reserved. Pages 15 (John), 18 (John), 23 (John), 25 (John, third paragraph), 27, 37 (John), 41 (John, first paragraph), 48 (John, first and third paragraphs), 53, 54 (John), 60 (John), 65 (John), 70 (John, first paragraph), 76, 79 (John), 86, 100 (John), 129 (John and Yoko), 131 (John), 139 (John), 145 (first three paragraphs), 147, 155 (Yoko), 169, 181 (Yoko, second paragraph), 181 (John, first and third paragraphs), 184 (John), 188 (John), 195, 206 (John, first paragraph), 213, 215 (second paragraph), 216 (John, first paragraph).

Interview for French television by François Vallee, March 1974. Courtesy of François Vallee. Pages 25 (John, first paragraph), 41 (John, second paragraph), 52 (John), 104.

Interview for KFRC RKO Radio by Dave Sholin, December 8, 1980. Courtesy of U.S. Radio Networks. Pages 25 (John, second paragraph), 125 (John), 155 (John), 157 (last John quote), 174, 187, 205, 206 (John, second and third paragraphs), 216 (John, bottom), 222 (John), 225, 229 (John), 232, 240, 242.

Interview by John Torv, February 1982. Courtesy of Andrew Solt Productions. Pages 32 (Allan Williams), 37 (Bob Wooler), 52 (George Martin, both), 60 (Paul McCartney), 100 (George Martin), 139 (George Martin).

From "The Mike Douglas Show," week of February 14, 1972. Courtesy of Group W Productions. Pages 48 (John, second paragraph), 120 (John).

Interview for KABC-TV by Elliot Mintz, November 1973. Courtesy of KABC-TV. Page 54 (Ringo Starr).

From "The Tomorrow Show" with Tom Snyder, April 1975. Courtesy of NBC Enterprises. Pages 63 (John), 157 (John, first paragraph), 172 (John, bottom).

Press Conference at Pan American Airlines, February 7, 1964. Courtesy of Universal Newsreel, Worldwide Television News Corporation. Page 65.

From "The Dick Cavett Show," September 24, 1971. Courtesy of Daphne Productions, Inc. Pages 70 (John, second paragraph), 135 (John, first paragraph), 172 (John, top).

From "Man of the Decade," ATV program, interview with Desmond Morris, December 30, 1969. Courtesy of ITC Entertainment Limited. Pages 74 (John), 145 (fourth paragraph).

Interview with John Lennon for BBC-TV, aired June 22, 1968. Courtesy of BBC Enterprises. Pages 74, 176 (first paragraph).

From "Twenty-Four Hours," aired December 15, 1969. Courtesy of BBC Enterprises. Pages 75 (John), 123 (John), 145 (bottom paragraph), 149 (John, first two paragraphs), 165.

Press conference in Chicago, August 1966. Courtesy of Worldwide Television News Corporation. Page 95 (John).

Interview by Tony Secunda, January 2, 1969. Courtesy of Tony Secunda. Pages 97 (John), 139 (Yoko), 157 (Yoko), 176 (second paragraph).

"The Lennon Tapes," interview by Andy Peebles for BBC Radio One, December 6, 1980. Courtesy of BBC Enterprises. Pages 99, 181 (John, second paragraph), 215 (first and third paragraphs).

Interview by Jonathan Cott for *Rolling Stone* magazine, December 5, 1980. Copyright © 1980 by Straight Arrow Publishers, Inc. Page 106.

Interview by Larry Kane, May 8, 1968. Courtesy of Stardust Productions. Page 129 (John and Paul).

Press Conference at Chateau Champlain, December 21, 1969. Courtesy of Tony Secunda and CBC-TV. Pages 135 (John, second paragraph), 176 (third paragraph).

From "The David Frost Show," June 7, 1969. Courtesy of BBC Enterprises. Pages 157 (John, second paragraph).

From *Mr. and Mrs. Lennon's Honeymoon,* film by John Lennon and Yoko Ono, week of March 23, 1969. Courtesy of Yoko Ono Lennon. Page 149 (John, bottom paragraph).

Interview by Abram Deswaan for Dutch television, October 1968. Courtesy of Deswaan Van Den Bos. Page 149 (Yoko).

From "The Way It Is" by Patrick Watson, June 1969. Courtesy of CBC. Page 166 (John).

Interview with John Lennon outside U.S. Immigration building, March 16, 1972. Courtesy of WCBS-TV. Pages 172 (John, middle paragraph), 177.

From "The Old Grey Whistle Test," April 18, 1975. Courtesy of BBC Enterprises. Page 176 (fourth and sixth paragraphs).

Interview with John Lennon, WCBS-TV, May 1972. Courtesy of Sherman Grinberg Film Libraries, Inc. Page 176 (fifth paragraph).

Interview by Maureen Cleave, March 4, 1966. Copyright © 1966 by the London *Evening Standard*. Page 93.

Sarah Lazin Books

Consulting Editor: Marianne Partridge

Photo Editor: Ilene Cherna Bellovin
Staff: Phil Bashe, Stephanie Franklin, Holly George, Amelie
Littell, Patricia Romanowski, Gila Sand, Laura Spencer

Art Director: Nancy Butkus
Designer: Robin Poosikian
Art Assistant: Brian Bowman

Production: Design and Printing Productions

The text is set in Garamond by A & S Graphics Inc.,
with display type in Weiss.

Printed and bound by W. A. Krueger, New Berlin, Wisconsin.